THE ARABS AND ISRAEL

TO JESSICA

The Arabs and Israel

A BACKGROUND BOOK

Charles Douglas-Home

DUFOUR

Dufour Editions, Inc.
Chester Springs, Pennsylvania 19425

© Charles Douglas-Home 1968
Library of Congress Catalog card number: 68–55233
Manufactured in Great Britain
First published in the U.S.A. 1968

CONTENTS

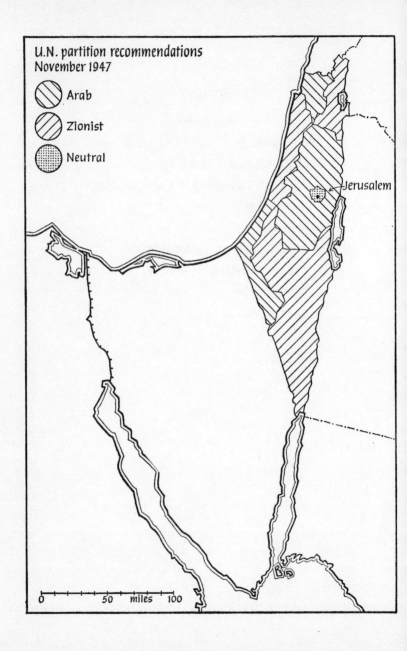

U.N. partition recommendations
November 1947

Arab

Zionist

Neutral

Jerusalem

0   50   miles   100

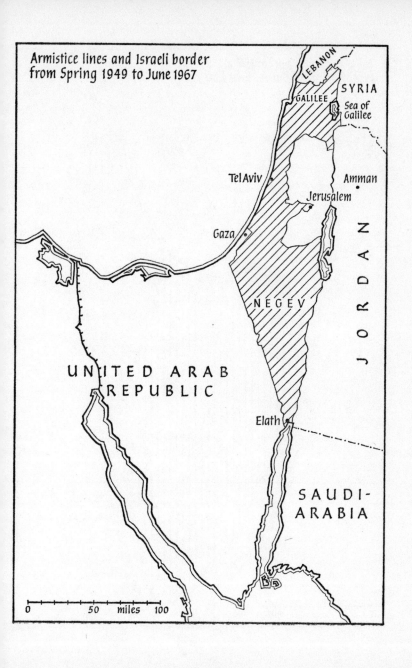

Armistice lines and Israeli border
from Spring 1949 to June 1967

LEBANON
SYRIA
GALILEE
Sea of Galilee
Tel Aviv
Amman
Jerusalem
Gaza
JORDAN
N E G E V
UNITED ARAB REPUBLIC
Elath
SAUDI-ARABIA

0   50   miles   100

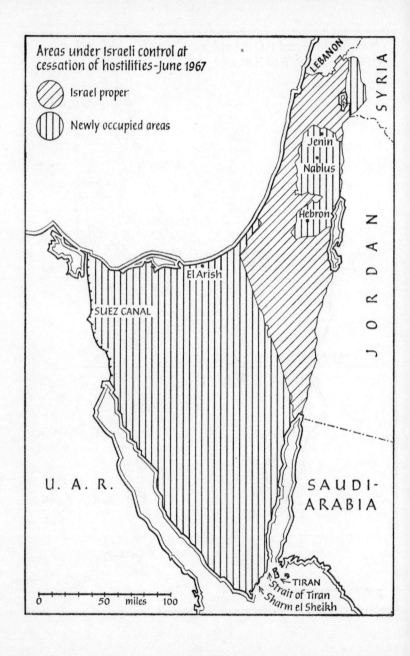

Areas under Israeli control at
cessation of hostilities-June 1967

Israel proper

Newly occupied areas

LEBANON

SYRIA

Jenin
Nablus
Hebron

JORDAN

El Arish

SUEZ CANAL

U. A. R.

SAUDI-
ARABIA

TIRAN
Strait of Tiran
Sharm el Sheikh

0   50   miles   100

INTRODUCTION

SINCE ISRAEL was declared a nation in May 1948 there have
been three wars between Israel and her Arab neighbours. With
each succeeding war Israel's military victory has been more convincing, and the Arab defeat more humiliating than on the previous occasion. Yet there is no sign that this generation of discord
is over.

Each war has brought about a changed situation. The first
brought the establishment of Israel, the second consolidated her
position, and the third brought her an empire. But there is no
finality about all this. A suspicion of good intentions on both
sides, an acknowledgement of the change of the balance of
power—all these attitudes are fashionable in the first flush of the
post-war period and gradually become eroded as the political
impossibilities in the Arab-Israel situation return.

The problem between Israel and the Arabs is a political one,
with no military solution. In fact the Middle East has had more
opportunities than most other areas of the world of discovering
once and for all that disputes cannot be solved simply by the
clash of arms. Yet the cycle of ignorance, or at least forgetfulness
of that compelling lesson, is a regrettably short one—much
shorter than in Europe, for instance, where the totality but the
irrelevance of war is fortunately a lesson which we in Europe
seem to be taking slightly longer to unlearn.

If the Arab-Israel dispute is more than a contest between
opposing armies—or even for that matter between opposing
societies with strong military orientation—what is it? It is important to get away from the actual belief that it is another symp-
tom of anti-semitism of the kind one might find in British or
American golf clubs. It is not specifically a product of racial
incompatibility between Arab and Jew. The history of Jewish

communities in the Arab world is not half so terrible as the history of Jewish tribulation at the hand of Christian or Communist European societies. It is fair to say that Jewish communities have probably flourished culturally and commercially with considerably more security in the Arab world over the last twenty centuries than they have in Europe.

Whatever the solution to the problem of Jewish assimilation into European societies, or acceptance by European societies of Jewish communities within their midst, it has nothing to do with the Palestine problem, nor indeed would many Jews have it otherwise. That is where a mistake is made, in confusing the two issues. Theodore Herzl made it originally when he founded the Zionist movement. Arthur Balfour, initiator of the Balfour Declaration, compounded it, but basically this confusion can be traced to its source in Zionism, and to the belief that the Middle East can absorb, without upheaval, the introduction of an almost totally new element.

I refer to the problem of Palestine because, although this book is really about the dispute between one nation—Israel—and her neighbours, the argument is over what should become of another nation—the now non-existent old Palestine.

It may appear to be preempting the question by saying that it involves the problem of what to do with the area originally called Palestine, and then referring to Israel, which occupies part of that area, as a sovereign factor in the matter. But one cannot study the problem of Palestine in a vacuum. There is a power situation in the area too, and one has got to accept the reality not only of Israel's right to exist—a right recognised by most of world opinion—but her *power* to exist. Israel has the power to exist in the face of this hostility but not the power to change that hostility without changing herself also. The point I wish to make is that Israel, which was the Jewish element in the Palestine question, has gone beyond being considered a subordinate, as opposed to a sovereign, element in the problem of the future of Palestine. It is too powerful for that.

It is therefore more a geopolitical than a racial problem, because the friction exists between states as power bodies—not as representatives of different races. The friction does not stem from the existence of an Arab–Jewish incompatibility such as one might say exists, far more noticeably, between Jews and Europeans—except in so far as European Jews in Israel tend to be out of sympathy both with Oriental Jews in that country and the Arab world in general.

The solution to the Arab–Israel problem therefore does not lie in the solution to the problem of world Jewry, but more in a local regional equilibrium between the states in the Middle East, of which Israel is one.

This book deals mainly with developments after the establishment of Israel as a state. The argument between her and the Arabs then became a contest between belligerent or quasi-belligerent sovereign states, rather than hostile communities.

Before the establishment of Israel, Palestine was a British responsibility and the argument was being conducted on many tiers and in many places not absolutely connected with the Middle East but often with domestic politics elsewhere, particularly in the United Kingdom and the United States. Although this still applies to outside countries who intervene or deem they should intervene in the area, the purpose of this book is to survey the dispute on the ground, as a power relationship, and not a moral one. Both sides are so absolutely convinced of the justice of their case that the moral view depends upon from which side you look at it. There would be little point, therefore, in making a moral judgment or seeking to award blame for any particular condition to either side.

The point of departure is 1948 because after that nobody else could claim to have real responsibility on the ground for whatever happened. It was at that date that the two contestants became primary powers in the argument, whereas before they had been secondary. Although Britain forfeited the control of events in Palestine before she departed, she had formal responsibility, and to that extent, therefore, events in Palestine were still largely dependent on her as the Mandatory power. After independence, Israel, certainly on the ground, was on her own just as the Arabs were basically on their own. Because the opposing parties to it were now more masters of the way they conducted the argument, the Arab–Zionist dispute was raised to the level of national politics.

A regional balance of power has been achieved, and although there have been changes, and may be others, the essential point is that the balance reflects the local power structure and is not one seriously affected by any outside power. No solution can now involve reversion to a situation when other people were responsible for the area—in other words before 1948. Besides, since any solution must in fact reflect a local balance, it would be like asking us to reclaim our Mandate, or asking the Turks to do so, or even asking the Romans to do so. One's frame of reference cannot really extend back beyond that point at which the present parties to any dispute assumed more or less total responsibility for it.

What that leaves one with may be a great wrong. In doing a great right for Zionism maybe Britain did a great wrong for the Arabs. Maybe that places upon Britain more responsibility to use her good offices and to understand that the parentage of the troubles is largely British. But with the end of our responsibility for the area came also the end of our power, and of our ability to intervene effectively in any situation there, although it finally took the Suez fiasco to convince us of this fact.

Sovereignty such as now achieved by Israel may not be formally recognised by the Arabs—as indeed is the case of East Germany where the West still argues that the Soviet armies keep that regime in power. But the West long ago accepted that we had neither the power nor the will, politically or militarily, to impose a solution on East Germany, but to hope that by induction the situation would improve. This may be basically what the Arabs feel about Israel, but the obvious difference is that periodically they start thinking they *do* have the will and the power to change the situation.

It is not that Israel exists which is really the cause of the dispute, but that in existing it helps to create conditions which the Arabs find intolerable. Admittedly, the nature of Arab rhetoric is such that the subtleties of this distinction can become lost. But that is not the point. If Israel existed as an Arab state there would be no dispute, except possibly between Israel and Jordan, over redemption of those areas of Palestine that had been annexed by Jordan after the 1948–1949 war.

In examining the Arab–Israel dispute between 1948 and 1967 one has to take into account the history of discord, and those long periods of strife before the foundation of Israel; maybe one can point to the British primary and American secondary responsibility for the state of Israel and for its emergence, possibly in expiation for the great crimes against Jewry which were committed in Europe, the extent of which has never been equalled by the Arabs themselves in all their history.

But all this background cannot disguise the fact that the situation between Israel and the Arabs is a power situation which no amount of moralising can alter if the powers themselves cannot, or do not wish to, alter it. It is against this background of a power relationship between the states that I have attempted to examine some of the specific issues which separate them, such as the refugee problem, the diversion of Jordan waters, frontier security, freedom of navigation, and so on. I have done this in the belief that although it is necessary to understand some of these points of contention it is only through an acknowledgement of the realities of the power background to the dispute that one can hope to establish some basis on which those differences themselves might be overcome.

I

From Palestine to Israel

PALESTINE is the area most closely linked with the history of three religions: Muslim, Jewish and Christian. Although its ancient history was closely involved with that of the Jewish people, the area came under Arab rule with the rise of Mohammed, and the Arabs then entered Palestine in sufficient numbers to have a serious effect on the ethnical make-up of the country. Before that it had been occupied by Byzantine forces, and before that had come under the rule of Rome.

The Jewish element had virtually disappeared with the sacking of Jerusalem in AD 70, when the dispersion began. Palestine under the Islamic rule formed part of the province of Syria, with which it has always been historically closely connected. It was part of the greater province of Syria and its fortunes fluctuated according to the fortunes of that province. Most of the prominent Arab families in Palestine of the 20th century first appeared as feudal lords during the first period of Ottoman rule in the 16th century.

Palestine is a loosely defined geographical area with little specific national tradition in its history. In the third quarter of the 18th century an Arab sheikh succeeded for a short time in establishing an independent principality in north Palestine in defiance of Ottoman authority, but the Turks soon crushed the rebellion. Palestine was later under Egyptian control for a while between 1832 and 1840, after which it reverted to direct Ottoman rule as an administrative province of Damascus. The first Jewish settlements to return to Palestine were brought in about 1855, and from then until 1914 these agricultural colonies increased until the Jewish population of the area was nearly 100,000 —still a decided minority compared to the Arabs, but certainly a noticeable one.

In fact they did not escape the unfavourable attentions of the Turks, who victimised the Jews during the Great War and caused

14

the Jewish population to drop, through emigration, to 50,000. With the assistance of the Arab rebellion against the Turks, British forces finally conquered the territory in 1917–1918, and a military administration was set up until 1920, when a civil one took over.

At the San Remo Conference of 1920 Britain was allotted the mandate for Palestine by her other allies. Thus Britain was in a position to feel acutely the contradictory effects of the promises which had been made to the Arabs and the Jewish Zionists during the first war. The first of these was in an exchange of letters between Sharif Hussein of Mecca (treated as the leading spokesman for the Arabs) and Sir Henry McMahon, British High Commissioner in Egypt.

The correspondence started in 1915 and in it Britain undertook with certain modifications to recognise and support the independence of the Arabs in all the regions within the limits demanded by the Sharif of Mecca, which stretched from Turkey to Aden and included Palestine. Shortly afterwards, the Sykes–Picot agreement was concluded between Britain and France, whereby the area formerly under Ottoman rule was to be carved up into spheres of influence, but Palestine was to have an international administration. Then a year later the Balfour Declaration of the British Government said, 'His Majesty's Government view with favour the establishment in Palestine of a national home for the Jewish people and will use their best endeavours to facilitate the achievement of that object, it being understood that nothing shall be done which may prejudice the civil and religious rights of non-Jewish communities in Palestine or the rights and political status enjoyed by Jews in any other country.'

This statement was the outcome of about twenty years' exchange of views between the British Government and Zionist leaders, during which various proposals had been considered for providing a home for the Jews. In addition to Palestine the proposals included Argentina, Uganda and the Sinai Desert. The movement to repatriate Jews to Palestine had been an old one among European Jewry, but it had no political impetus until Theodore Herzl, an Austrian journalist, founded the first Zionist Congress in 1897. Even then, the idea of actual statehood for the Jews was not positive, and Herzl himself seldom went further than thinking in terms of a Jewish community safeguarded as such by laws.

The Basel Programme, after the 1897 Congress, said that the aim of Zionism was to create for the Jewish people a home in Palestine, secured by public law. In order to obtain this objective, the Zionist Congress adopted the following means: 'The systematic promotion of the settlement of Palestine with Jewish agriculturists, partisans and craftsmen; the organisation and federation of all Jewry by means of local and general institutions in conformity with the local laws; the strengthening of Jewish sentiment and national consciousness; preparatory steps for securing such Government assents as are necessary for achieving the object of Zionism.'

After the publication of the Balfour Agreement, Britain reassured Sharif Hussein that the idea of an independent Jewish state in Palestine was not contemplated, but that the Government were determined that no obstacle should be put in the way of Jewish repatriation to Palestine as far as was compatible with the freedom of the existing population—who were Palestinian Arabs. The mandate embodied in one of its articles terms for the establishment of a Jewish national home in Palestine while ensuring that the rights and position of the other sections of the population were not prejudiced. The mandate was formally confirmed by the League of Nations in 1923.

The real rivalry between Arabs and Jews only started after the Balfour Declaration, but the declaration as such did not start it. With the award of the mandate Britain was in a position to carry out the Declaration and, more important, was in a position to be forced to fulfil the essentially incompatible promises which had been made to Jews and Arabs alike about the future of Palestine.

The dispute was about the future of Palestine in its broadest context. Where any fundamental change in the ethnic balance of Palestine was likely to change the country completely, then obviously consideration of race became predominant, particularly as Britain was the only power in the area at the time. The actual power relationship of the communities could not really be tested while Britain presided over law and order in the area. Therefore their divisions, although destined later to be put to the test in a power struggle, nevertheless took on the contemporary hue of a racial dispute.

The 'double promised' land, as it came to be called as a result of Britain's ambiguous undertakings to Arabs and Jews, was only doubly promised if one put a particular interpretation on the Balfour Declaration. It was a question as to whether it was to be *a* national home or *the* national home. If a Jewish national home meant simply a guaranteed community with minority rights under the overall control of the Arabs—who would presumably see to it that the extent of such a home did not damage the interests of the existing population—then it was likely to be a pretty small national home. Presumably most Jews thought this too, because by 1929 Jewish immigration to Palestine had tailed off and at that time total Jewish immigration to Palestine would probably not have expanded outside the limits of Arab tolerance. It was not until the European persecutions of the 1930s that Jewish immigration picked up, and with it the possibility of Palestine becoming not only a national home for the Jews, but rising to Jewish statehood in the process.

Of course that possibility had always been the objective of the Zionists. Although they did not represent all Jews by any means —indeed they caused profound distress among many more or less assimilated Jewish communities—by dint of extreme activism, relentless diplomacy and brilliant timing, they managed to keep the idea of statehood alive in the lean years, and so were quite able to catch the tide of sympathy which swept in as a result of the Jewish persecutions of the 1930s.

There is no need to trace every development in the growth of Zionism from its origins in the late 19th century and its transformation from a luminous idea to practical statehood over not more than sixty years. It survived through a combination of shrewdness, skullduggery, influence in high places skilfully deployed, vision, propaganda, terrorism, and indecision in Whitehall, not to mention luck and the absence of many of those qualities among the Arab leadership at the time.

Local leadership of the Arabs in Palestine was to some extent provided by the Mufti of Jerusalem, but the overall support provided for him by the other Arabs was only skin deep, since, if they had been asked to say what sort of Palestine they were hoping for, their answers would have exposed the basic rivalry between the Hashemites and the rest. The former were the two monarchies, Transjordan and Iraq, who saw the future of Palestine basically as an extension of the Kingdom of Transjordan. The latter, Egypt, Syria and Saudi Arabia, were solely united in their desire to prevent the former realising this ambition, but with no very articulate view of what sort of Palestine should be there in its stead. It was more their hostility to the Hashemites which accounted for their support of the Mufti than any genuine belief in the future of an independent Palestine led by him or his family.

The trouble with Zionism is that it has never really defined the limits of Jewish penetration, particularly if one recalls historically the extent to which Zionism was conceived at a time when there were no national frontiers in that area, but simply the administrative provinces of the Ottoman empire. The trouble now is that the carve-up which followed the Arab rebellion and the defeat of the Turks in the first World War resulted in new states being formed by the signing of the Treaty of Versailles.

So the early imaginative base for Zionism thereafter came across national frontiers where before there had been nothing so specific. There has been no real attempt, however, to redefine Zionism in the light of the 1920 settlement, and there is no doubt that that expansive nature of Zionism, particularly when combined with the number of Jews in the dispersion referred to by Zionism (twelve million) and the obviously limited absorptive capacity of the area, all cause concern to the Arabs, who assume that somebody will have to make way if all Zionist conditions are fulfilled.

Indeed, the earlier expansion of Zionism was confirmed in 1942 at a conference of Zionists in a New York hotel which passed the Biltmore Resolution. The resolution demanded that 'Palestine be established as a Jewish Commonwealth' with control of her own immigration and the development of all unoccupied and uncultivated lands in the country. Although the resolution was the subject of much internal argument among American Jews, it was subsequently adopted by the central executive of the Jewish agency in Palestine, and thus became official policy of the body from which the first government of the state of Israel emerged.

As a result of the persecution of the 1930s however, Jewish immigration under the mandate increased to half-a-million by 1939—one-third of the total population in Palestine. It was stimulated more by European persecution than by the authority of Zionism. World opinion was appalled at the European situation and clutched eagerly at the suggestion that the Jewish refugee problem could be solved in Palestine. Arab hostility was not articulated or intellectually organised to cope with this combination. There were new intellectual forces in the Arab world for sure, but without the concentration of effort or unity of purpose and consistency which characterised the Zionist leadership. Lack of British sympathy for the Arabs in the early 1930s, coupled with the increased Jewish immigration, became the signal for continuous Arab protests which culminated in the rebellion between 1936 and 1939. This was in the end firmly suppressed by British troops.

Before that the British Government had tottered and oscillated between one Royal Commission report and another; between sympathy for the Jews and sympathy for the Arabs. The passion for impartiality had the same inequitable result in the Mandate, where impartiality—equal obligation—was actually no match for the immensely superior mettle of the Jews over the Arabs. British impartiality more or less allowed them to sort it out themselves, with occasional twinges of authority to restore the balance when things looked too bad or when the effects on Britain's external relations with the Arab world called for redress.

Of such was the White Paper of 1939, which put a definite ceiling of 75,000 on Jewish immigration between 1939 and 1945, with numbers thereafter to be decided by the Arabs. The White Paper—inhuman though it was in terms of the refugees from

Europe being turned away—nevertheless reflected the reality of the approaching war and the fact that the British Government could not afford not to do something to assure as much Arab support as possible against the Axis powers, support which the Palestine situation had threatened to undermine.

Nevertheless, the White Paper had few long term effects on the future of Palestine, and when, after the war, both Jews and Arabs rejected the idea of any further trusteeship, Britain referred the whole matter back to the UN in February 1947. The United Nations Special Committee on Palestine recommended partition of Palestine as between a Jewish state and an Arab state in economic union, with an international city of Jerusalem in the middle. The Jews accepted it and the Arabs did not. In fact at a later date the Arabs wanted to accept it in retrospect, or at least said that the position should be restored to what had been proposed in the partition report. But by then the Israelis would not.

The events immediately following the declaration of the state of Israel, the first Arab–Israeli war and the armistice agreements of 1949 will be dealt with later. But it is worth noting the principles enshrined in the proposed partition, because they have the authority of the United Nations, and at one time or other both Arab and Israeli have formally recognised the UN's authority to make such a judgment.

Always accepting that they have come to these individual conclusions at different times, it is nevertheless still relevant, because it makes this partition report one of the few meeting points. What it shows is that they have both at certain times recognised the UN authority in deciding the future of Palestine. Whereas there is no need to go into the detailed geography of that partition report, their acceptance would seem to underwrite, therefore, the general principles of the United Nations Report, and these are important.

The report recognises the existence of both Jewish and Arab communities in Palestine. It acknowledged Palestine as an area distinct from the other states around it, which were Transjordan, Egypt, Lebanon and Syria. And it admitted two states within the purview of Palestine. The difference really centres on the connection between racial entity and nationhood, and the necessity or not for each racial entity within Palestine to be elevated to the individual level of a state.

It is true that Arab-Jewish feelings at that time really prohibited the idea of partnership with one state, but the actual principle of a bi-national state was being well observed next door in the Lebanon between Muslim and Christian. Perhaps the most emphatic part of the UN report was in the distinction it made between a home for the Jewish people and *the* home. Since, as we have seen, the state of Israel partially credits its legitimacy to the UN recommendations of 1947, the relevant language of the report merits quotation. It recommended that 'In the appraisal of the Palestine question, it be accepted as incontrovertible that any solution for Palestine cannot be considered as a solution of the Jewish problem in general', and then went on to make the following comments:

'(a) Palestine is a country of limited area and resources. It already has a considerable settled population which has an unusually high rate of natural increase. It is, therefore, most improbable that there could be settled in Palestine all the Jews who may wish to leave their present domiciles, for reasons of immediate displacement or distress, or actual or anticipated anti-Jewish attitudes in the countries in which they now reside.
'(b) In any case, owing to the factors of time, limited transportation and local ability to absorb, it could not be anticipated that Palestine alone could relieve the urgent plight of all the displaced and distressed Jews.
'(c) Further, serious account must be taken of the certain resentment and vigorous opposition of the Arabs throughout the Middle East to any attempt to solve, at what they regard as their expense, the Jewish problem, which they considered to be an international responsibility. . . .'*

Differentiation between Zionism and a Zionist-Israel state on the one hand and a 'de-Zionised' Israel on the other, between *a* national home and *the* national home for the Jews, was evidently one of the basic principles of the UN approach to the problem.

*(Vol. 1 p. 46, Lake Success, New York, 1947.)

From that distinction, of course, many other questions follow. If Israel as a state is not designed to be exclusively for Jews but merely for a Jewish community in the Arab world, does that automatically require a Jewish majority, and if so what kind of a majority, to ensure the security and continuity of a Jewish tradition in the Middle East?

Moreover, what is likely to be the effect on other Middle East societies of the introduction of this community? These questions go to the root of the Arab–Israeli problem. It is fair to say that the UN partition report, in making its distinctions, recognised the dangers, but in the hysterical atmosphere of the end of the Mandate few other people seem to have been ready or willing to do so.

On the day Britain left Palestine—May 14, 1948—Ben Gurion declared the establishment of the state of Israel. The new country was recognised immediately by the United States, after three days by the Soviet Union, after three weeks by the United Nations, and only after ten months by Britain. The criteria adopted by those countries who offered immediate recognition are political ones, since recognition is granted or withdrawn as a political act, whereas the traditional British criterion has always been the physical ability of a regime to control its designated territory and show itself master at least of its internal destiny. This presumably could not be absolutely guaranteed until the outcome of the Arab–Israeli War, which followed Ben Gurion's declaration, was more certain.

The Arab armies marched on Israel the moment the establishment of the state was declared. As always, the Arab strategy was piecemeal because there was no consensus about what the Arab world actually wanted to do with the area they called Palestine. It was clear that King Abdullah of Jordan both wanted, and was prepared to take, the Arab-occupied areas of Palestine and absorb them into his kingdom, and this task was certainly made easier by the efficiency of the Arab Legion troops, who had British officers, and by the almost active encouragement of the British Government. — how relate to my topic?

A determination to prevent Abdullah succeeding in this was as much the other Arabs' motive as any genuine desire to Arabise

22

the whole of Palestine, and their sympathy with the Mufti and his plans for an Arab-Palestine was as much motivated by their dislike of Abdullah's plans as their belief that a state of Palestine under the Mufti was either a possibility or even a satisfactory solution. As it was, and in fact still is, the Arab strategy was non-existent, but at the time their initial superiority to Israel, numerically and in terms of equipment, managed to conceal the effects of this strategic vacuum so that the final outcome of the war was not certain for some months.

The most important battle and certainly the one which commanded most of the world attention was the battle for communications to Jerusalem. The emotional and psychological factors were quite as important as the tactical ones where Jerusalem was concerned—and that applies to both sides—and the fighting was most fierce and the losses per acre won were the most disheartening in the Jerusalem sector. Israel lost the Jewish quarter in the walled city of Jerusalem but held on to other parts. Eventually, however, Israel had to build a new road from Tel Aviv to Jerusalem, since the old road led through Latrun, which is situated on a knuckle of land which remained held by Jordan until the 1967 campaign. The second most important battles were being fought against the Egyptian Army in the Negev Desert to the south and between Beersheba and Jerusalem. The Lebanese in the north made no real intervention, but just an appearance, and the Syrians were halted sharply in north-eastern Galilee with little gains. Iraq sent soldiers into Jordan, but they were defeated at a crossing of the Jordan river, and although they made a further advance westwards their intervention was never, after this, highly significant.

The fighting was anyway almost beyond all the belligerents' resources, and after about three weeks the UN mediator, Count Bernadotte, arranged a four-week truce at the beginning of June. He tried to prolong the truce, and everybody except Egypt and Syria appeared to be keen to do so, exhausted as they were by the war. But those two countries insisted on an immediate resumption of hostilities; they were caught on a wave of propaganda from which there was no return. In fact their strategies, here and often again in the course of the next twenty years, were to be dictated more by the uncontrollable nature of the propaganda monster which they had created than by any analytical or considered appreciation of the sort of approach they should be considering.

When the four-week truce ended in July there were ten days of fierce fighting during which Israel established her position in most of northern Galilee and broke through to Jerusalem. The Arabs gained positions in Gaza and made some advances in southern Galilee. This spasm was ended by a second Security Council truce. Thereafter, Count Bernadotte attempted to persuade both sides to agree to a compromise, and in the course of his work he came under criticism from Jewish Ministers, and more or less as a result of this he was murdered by the Stern Gang of Jewish extremists on September 17. Meanwhile on October 1, King Abdullah of Jordan had assumed sovereignty over Arab Palestine in spite of an earlier claim by the Mufti that he alone represented the Government of Palestine.

By now Israel was ready for the third phase of fighting, with an army which had doubled its strength and profited by the arms supplies from Czechoslovakia. (The second wave of Arab-Israel fighting eight years later was directly attributed by Israel to another Czech arms deal, only this time to the other side. There is some talk that the deal in 1956 was in fact a Russian one under Czech auspices, but whether or not that was so, one cannot really condemn it unless one is prepared also to condemn the earlier shipments in 1948 to Israel.)

In mid-October the Israeli and Egyptian armies were once again at war in the Negev Desert, and Israel captured Beersheba on October 21. On the next day the new UN mediator, Dr Bunche, arranged another truce. To the north, however, there was a renewed bout of fighting the next week and Israel captured the rest of Galilee. Skirmishing broke out again in the Negev about two months later, when Israel consolidated her position and this finally led to the armistice agreement being signed with Egypt on February 24. The treaty with Jordan was signed on April 3 with a clause in it covering Iraq's withdrawal as well. The Lebanon had signed on March 23 and Syria was to sign much later on July 29, mainly because of domestic political uncertainties.

Between the signing of the treaty with Egypt and the one with Jordan, Israel captured the port of Eilat on the coast of the Gulf of Aqaba and the Egyptians have claimed since then that this was an illegal act since it was after the armistice. The Israel counter-argument holds that Eilat was never disputed territory between Israel and Egypt, but only in dispute with Jordan and that the armistice with Jordan was not signed until after the day of Eilat's capture. In theory the Egyptian case could be countered by saying that they do not apply a similar recognition to Israeli-occupied areas in the north which might have been established after the Israel-Egypt ceasefire, and it is anyway worth remembering that Eilat was awarded to Israel in the UN partition scheme.

Thus at the end of sporadic fighting lasting less than a year Israel was established and the Arabs had accepted this fact in their negotiations under the UN auspices on the island of Rhodes.

The areas that had once been Palestine and had not been conquered by Israel now came under the control of either Jordan or Egypt. Egypt always observed the legal distinction between the Gaza strip, over which she was awarded provisional control by the general armistice agreement, and the remaining territory in Sinai. Gaza has never been part of Egypt, so that the refugees collected therein had no claim on Egyptian citizenship. The situation was quite different with regard to Jordanian-held Palestine, which was completely absorbed into the Kingdom of Jordan, and the refugees there were granted Jordanian citizenship as well.

However, it was fully accepted at the time of the armistice agreements that the boundaries were not political boundaries, but simply lines of truce drawn on the map and regarded as lines beyond which forces were not allowed to move.

For military reasons (which were not always justifiable in terms of security needs) Israel imposed fairly harsh frontier conditions on the Arab world, so that the frontier frequently separated Arabs from their land. The Arab situation on the land is very different from Israel. In Israel the entire country is covered by a network of villages called Nahal settlements and the planning of a village and its agricultural area is conceived first of all as a security unit so that the kind of separation involved with the Arabs could never happen to an Israel settlement.

One would have thought that the sheer irrationalities of some of the armistice lines would have made it obvious to most people that they would not last for ever, although as the years went by they seemed to become more and more fixed. However, the parties to the armistice agreements never really seemed to understand the short-term nature of the agreement and the fact that the Israel lines were dictated exclusively by military considerations and were valid only for the period of the armistice. In spite of this, they all agreed not to change them by force or to resort to force; no aggressive action was to be planned and each state was to respect the other's security.

2

Frontiers, Terrorism and Propaganda

ALTHOUGH THE frontiers had been temporarily settled in the armistice agreements in 1949, terrorism soon started up again. But it would be a mistake to attribute the incessant fighting on Israel–Arab frontiers only, or even mainly, to the unnatural demarcation lines which had been agreed. Although they obviously provided an encouragement, they were not the root of the trouble. The frontier problem was simply an expression of a wider and deeper political division between the two blocks, and because the frontiers were indeed illogical, and in some cases almost untenable, it obviously made it easier for the Arabs to express their general political dissatisfaction in frontier incidents than in other subtler but less noticeable ways.

The dispute in fact was concerned with many issues other than the delineation of frontiers, which itself has never really been of central importance to either side. But it is interesting to see how the essentially incidental or indirect aspect of frontier pressure eventually boomeranged on all concerned and, although frontier security did not start as a main element, because of Israeli strategy it soon became very hard to divorce it from the other political elements of the dispute. One might assume that frontier incidents have always been the currency of Arab dissatisfaction and an indirect expression of their inability to exert any more purposeful pressure on Israel—an expression almost of frustration. Israel on the other hand, confident of her military superiority, has time and again modelled her frontier strategy in a military context isolated from the other political factors. The Arabs insistence on treating the refugee and Jordan waters problems as central issues on the one hand, and on the other hand, Israel's relegation of those matters to secondary place when compared with the problem of security, have from the start reflected the basically incompatible approaches of the two sides. The more they argued about the priorities for a settlement, the more they over-emphasised their own attitudes, and the harder each position became.

Terrorism was resumed from Arab countries soon after the 1949 agreements, and carried on spasmodically until there was a sharp deterioration after the early months of 1955. Each act of terrorism provoked a more serious Israeli retaliation. Basically their strategy is supposed to be reprisal at military rather than civilian targets, but this is a rather variable yardstick, since although the Israeli Army would always plan to strike at military objectives in the territory from which the terrorism had come there was not always a target lucrative enough (or available) to drive the message home. It would not be correct to say absolutely that whereas Arab terrorism concerned civilians, Israel reprisals were directed exclusively at the military. The civilians lost out both ways.

What is terrorism? In the 50,000 odd incidents which have been the subject of Israeli and Arab complaints to the UN, (30,000 Israeli complaints, 20,000 from the Arabs) almost every variety is covered. A complaint from the machine gunning of tractor drivers, or farm labourers, to the mining of bridges or culverts, or booby traps on footpaths. Most terrorist acts worked on the hit and run principle, the terrorists themselves taking advantage of the available sanctuary behind the frontier. And it was the sanctity of this sanctuary which Israeli reprisals had to disprove. The communiqués after most of these incidents refer disingenuously to tracks of footprints being found from the scene of the minelaying to the nearest frontier. I personally find this always rather hard to believe, as the territory seldom really favours that kind of tracking, even if the terrorists would be so elementary as to leave their mark. But it is worth quoting a passage written by General Dayan—the former Israel Chief of Staff, and at the time of writing Israel Defence Minister—on the subject of Israel's retaliatory policy because in it he reveals the basic inflexibility about such a posture. The strategy shows up if anything, only the fundamental lack of sublety in the military mind. The American bombing of North Vietnam is based on the principle of raising the price of aggression at source. It is an exactly similar attitude to that of the Israeli military, without holding out any more hopeful sign of an eventual solution to the problem of frontier security. In his book on the Suez Campaign, General Dayan explained the policy of retaliation as follows:

'The purpose was to show the Arabs that while Israel might be unable to protect the life of every tractor driver ploughing the field close to the border or prevent mining of dirt approach tracks to an immigrant village, the country responsible for the saboteurs would not get off scot free. When an Israeli force operated inside Arab territory without the local armies being able seriously to challenge them, the Arab military failure was openly demonstrated to their own people. Thus, instead of raising the prestige of the Arab regimes, the net result of Fedayun actions was to shake popular trust in them and in their armed forces.'*

The Arabs were presented with a choice either to raise the stakes or abandon the course of action. The inevitability of Israel's reply meant that the Arabs could and did strengthen their forces in readiness to cushion such a blow. This meant that every minor foray escalated into an armed battle.

Of course from the Israeli point of view it was less easy to know how else to counteract this type of irritation. The frontier attacks stemmed from Arab dissatisfaction with the political background of the whole dispute, and from their impotence to do anything more about it than annoy Israel at this pinprick level. Thus Israel had a choice: she could either accept the Arab case that there was some cause for political dissatisfaction, and therefore make some political gesture in the hope that it would assuage Arab dissatisfaction enough for them to discontinue the attacks; or she could reject the political basis for the Arab dissatisfaction, reject the idea that there was any possibility of a wider justification for the frontier attacks, and punish the offenders accordingly.

The danger in the situation arose because both sides were convinced of their rights. Neither was physically strong enough to assert that right to a conclusion of the dispute. The Arabs were

*Dayan: *Diary of the Sinai Campaign*. Steinatzky, 1965.

29

not weak enough to be destroyed by Israel yet they were far from being strong enough themselves to destroy Israel. Israel on the other hand, while being strong enough to make every retaliation hurt, was not strong enough to make it hurt so much that the Arabs would not do it again. In this enormously expansionary phase of nation-building, when Israel was hoping all the time to attract new immigrants, and hang on to them, it was also very important to see that life was made as secure as possible in the new country. Whatever the social security being offered to Jewish immigrants to Israel, they were not likely to be encouraged to remain in a country where there was a constant danger of being sniped at, or mined in the frontier areas. Fear of losing their population, as much as anything else in Israel's attitude, accounted for the relatively short periods of patience before a frontier incident had to be decisively avenged.

It is also worth mentioning Israel's attitude towards the UN in the light of this policy, because whereas the presence of a UN force would certainly have stopped and detected any large-scale Israeli reprisal, it would not have been very likely to stop the Arab attacks, which were less easy to detect. If the vigilance of Israel could not detect it, the UN could hardly do so. Israel, with or without a UN screen, would obviously have been just as vulnerable as before, without being able to strike back in the manner to which she had become accustomed.

As the years wore on, the Israel response was actually widened to cover more indirect attacks from the Arabs, and not only as a response to infringements of frontier security. Arab frontier terrorism in fact seldom took place in a vacuum but more against a background of overall political pressure on Israel, and only reflected dissatisfaction because that political pressure was largely unavailing. The pressure was coupled and indeed encouraged by propaganda, and propaganda on both sides soon saw to it that the political dispute and the frontier terrorism were both magnified into major issues of national security.

As the terrorism went on, so the scale of reprisal became larger, and so the affront against the Arabs became more insupportable. As this led to more terrorism and more extravagant assertions that they, the Arabs, would win through in the end, there followed more extravagant assertions from Israel that they would not lose. This exaggeration was translated into dangerous political attitudes; Israel came to interpreting every frontier incursion, every manifestation of the Arab economic boycott, as a matter of national survival; yet her continued ability to outlive these threats and not to modify her policies was regarded as an unacceptable affront by the entire Arab world.

The armistice agreements had not created a state of peace. Egyptian prize courts were still sitting, and the Government in Cairo ignored a UN Security Council resolution in September 1951 which called on Egypt to end the state of belligerence and lift the blockade. After 1953 discrimination against Israeli shipping started to become worse, and Egypt banned the passage through the Straits of Tiran of all goods in Israeli ships, even non-military cargoes and even non-military vessels.

In September 1954 Egypt seized an Israeli ship on the south end of the Canal and returned the sailors only after three months in prison. Finally in September 1955 all airline companies were required to give 72 hours warning of flights over Sinai and then El Al (the Israeli airline) was forbidden to fly there at all, thus stopping expanding traffic to Africa.

The first nine months of 1955 produced 153 killed and wounded Israelis from terrorist attacks. Ben Gurion the Israeli Prime Minister, proposed to the Cabinet in November 1955 to take action, but he was overruled as the time was not thought to be propitious. In December 1955 General Dayan urged that Israel must recapture the Straits of Tiran within one month. Otherwise, he argued, the fact that Israel continued to sit with Egypt on the Mixed Armistice Commission would be regarded as a de facto surrender of her rights in the Gulf of Aqaba whereas the embargo should be regarded a unilateral break of the armistice agreement by Egypt.

This recommendation illustrates acutely the Israeli dilemma, and at the same time the artificial nature of the threat. There was no suggestion, in reality, that the embargo on shipping to Eilat at that time constituted a serious economic threat to the future of Israel. Of course it was an inconvenience, but it is clear from

Dayan's recommendation that it was not so much the act of closure, which incidentally was not so obviously illegal as one imagines, that roused Dayan to action, but the fact that unless action was taken, and as long as Israel and Egypt continued to sit together on the MAC which had been set up as a result of the armistice, this would be taken as passive acceptance of Egypt's rights to do what she liked. This position has an uncanny echo in the Israeli attitude adopted in 1967. Nevertheless, General Dayan's recommendation was eventually adopted and resulted in the second Arab-Israeli war—the Suez campaign of 1956.

According to General Dayan there were really three causes of the Israeli expedition to Suez. They were the Egyptian preparations for all-out war, as illustrated by their receipt of Czech arms; the increase in terrorism from 1955 onwards; and the gradual throttling of Israeli traffic up and down the Gulf of Aqaba. Before the Suez campaign Eilat was receiving only a few thousand tons of cargo and there could not be said to be any real economic threat to Israel at that stage arising out of the troubles with traffic through the Gulf. The campaign was, of its kind, a major retaliatory action by Israel, involving a whole host of psychological and political factors as well as the economic one, which, after all, had been on the shelf for twelve months since General Dayan first recommended action.

The campaign was all over in a few days. By then Israel had captured the Sinai peninsula, freed the Gulf of Aqaba and remained in positions ten miles to the east of the Suez Canal. The diplomatic negotiations which followed on from this campaign succeeded in confusing the essential issues of the Arab–Israel confrontation, at least to start with, because of the Anglo-French intervention into Egypt. But there are some remarkable similarities between the situation then and the situation which followed on from the 1967 campaign. Israel was in possession of occupied territory, and, for instance, her Foreign Minister, Mrs Golda Meir, stated immediately after the campaign that the Gaza Strip was part of Israeli territory. The Syrian Army said it was receiving arms from the Communists because of the unacceptable conditions attached to any Western arms. Israel stated that Egyptians would not be allowed to return to Gaza. Egypt, Saudi

Arabia and Syria agreed to supply Jordan with money and arms. Israel informed the UN Secretary-General in January 1957 that her forces would not be withdrawn from Gaza or the Gulf of Aqaba without binding guarantees that these areas would not be used for future Egyptian hostilities against Israel. These demands were rejected by Hammarskjold the UN Secretary-General. The next month the Secretary of State, Mr Dulles, wrote an aide-memoire to the Israeli Ambassador to the United States containing the following statement:

'In the absence of some overriding decisions to the contrary, as by the International Court of Justice, the United States on behalf of vessels of United States registry is prepared to exercise the right of free and innocent passage and to join with others to secure general recognition of this right.'

He also offered a plan whereby Israel would withdraw her forces from the Gulf of Aqaba in exchange for United States influence to establish that the Straits of Tiran were an international waterway, and the establishment of a UN trusteeship over Gaza. Egypt denounced this plan and Israel rejected it while promising to resettle some of the Arab refugees in Israel. On February 17, 1957, Israel declared that any one of three alternatives would be sufficient to guarantee the removal of Israeli troops from Egyptian territory: (1) a guarantee from any major world power that any Egyptian blockade of Aqaba would not be tolerated, (2) the stationing of a UN force at Sharm el Sheikh (the mouth of the Gulf of Aqaba) to ensure freedom of passage, or (3) an agreement among the nations bordering the Gulf (including Egypt) which would permit the free passage of the ships of all nations. The United States replied, in a White House statement, by indicating to Israel that actions already taken by the United Nations, plus assurances from the United States and other governments, provided Israel 'with the maximum assurance that it can reasonably expect at this juncture, or that can be reconciled with fairness to others'.

Shortly afterwards, on March 4, Ben Gurion ordered the Israeli army to withdraw from the Gaza Strip and the Gulf of Aqaba. Students in Jerusalem demonstrated against this order.

Three weeks later, the French Premier, M. Mollet, said that France would stand behind Israel's right to use force to block any Egyptian attack either against Israeli shipping in the Gulf of Aqaba or launched from the Gaza Strip. The USSR warned of retaliation if France and Israel attacked Egypt. Under an interim arrangement between the UN and Egypt, the UN began forming a Palestine-Arab police force for joint patrolling of the Gaza strip. In April, Israel agreed to a barbed wire fence and minefield barrier between her territory and the Gaza strip, and UN forces were stationed in Gaza and at Sharm el Sheikh.

The Suez expedition brought about some major political changes in the area as well as peace to Israel's frontiers. Although the Arab League announced plans for further boycotting of Israeli goods, the Arabs were weaker and divided and took to propaganda attacks on each other rather than on Israel. But there was little permanent change in the basic elements of the dispute. Although there was a noticeable decrease in terrorism for some time, Ben Gurion said in 1958 that the events in the Arab world such as the coup in Iraq and the establishment of the UAR had increased the encirclement of Israel, and warned Israel to continue to be on her guard.

The arming of both sides in the Middle East continued apace during the period following the Suez war. Officially the three Western powers—Britain, France and the United States—had agreed in 1950 not to sell arms which would upset the balance of power in the area. The spirit of this agreement was first broken by the French who sold jet aircraft to Israel after Suez. Britain then proceeded to sell tanks to Israel and Iraq and jet fighter bombers to Jordan. The United States sold tanks to Jordan and the Soviet Union gradually took over as the main supplier of arms and aircraft to Egypt and Syria and subsequently Iraq. This expansion in the fire power of all concerned spelt inevitable danger when combined with the prevailing strategic attitudes of both Israel and the Arabs.

In the early days of primitive armies, scantily organised and ill-equipped, the tradition of resorting to fighting without giving the normal diplomatic process much time to take the steam out of any situation may have been all very well. Unfortunately it carried over into the 1960s when the military capability of the two sides made such a cavalier approach to the question of fighting increasingly dangerous. It did not seem, however, to provoke any change in the strategic thinking of either side.

The Arabs still professed their intention to eliminate Israel. The Israelis still proved their ability to punish the Arabs hard for the frontier incursions. Both appeared to be unaware of the absurdity of allowing so close a link to be made between large scale jet-age warfare and political differences which they had already lived with for nearly a generation, without any fundamental threat to their basic securities.

The many years of retaliation for frontier incidents and of listening to Arab incantations about her destruction were not without effect on Israel. A siege mentality developed. Israel slipped into the habit of half-believing Arab propaganda, and half-accepting the view held in certain French and British colonial circles that all the Arab understands is force. An analysis of inter-Arab affairs, say between Egypt, Jordan, Iraq and Syria, would surely contradict this view that the currency of Arab diplomacy is essentially a military one. But that was certainly the view from Tel Aviv. And it had led to the formulation of a politico-military philosophy which would be a dangerous one for any country to adopt, particularly in the circumstances in which Israel has found herself in the nuclear age.

Her philosophy is this. Her position is so threatened in the long term that, even though individual actions by those who threaten do not necessarily amount to much in the short term, they have to be treated as seriously as the total threat, because to ignore them would encourage the adversaries to advance a next step and so on and so on, until the extinction of Israel is achieved. This philosophy is as much applied to political acts by Israel's Arab neighbours as to their military behaviour. General Rabin gave a full explanation of it in 1965 when making a speech about the diversion of Jordan's water, which Israel incidentally prevented happening by bombing attacks on the construction whenever the work appeared to be getting too advanced.

He said, 'We must rid ourselves of outdated concepts of international hostility. There are people whose concept of aggression only applies to acts perpetrated by means of arms and man-slaughter. If diversion should succeed it will have a serious bearing on the Arab feelings of action (feelings generated by a non-response to their operation). This creates a climate that makes for greater licence and in which soldiers might be more ready to shoot at targets of opportunity.'

It can be seen that he was justifying military action, much as General Dayan had justified it ten years earlier, before Suez, on the grounds that the psychological effect of not fighting (feelings generated by a non-response) would only encourage the Arabs to do more.

Israel had thus ruled out the possibility of any sort of nego-tiation with the Arabs. The dialogue was a military one or it was nothing. General Rabin went on in the same speech to explain that Israel hoped her policy of retaliation would deter the Arabs from trying anything or attempting to obtain changes in the balance of power in their favour. Then he appeared to show up the weakness of this position, however, when he said, 'If in the midst of a campaign for the very life of the state of Israel, she has nevertheless not been attacked out of fear of her military power, our deterrent capacity has fulfilled its mission.' Of course it had not. It had not satisfied the Arabs that there was no more to be gained against Israel in their dispute. It had simply per-suaded them that there was nothing to be gained by attempting a frontal assault on Israel.

The policy of deterrence, of instant retaliation, paid no atten-tion to the fact that there were an infinite number of aspects to the dispute which could not be worked out in terms of military security, and Arab pressures which could not be answered by shooting back. How, for instance, could Israel justify her view that she would be justified in immediately going to war with Jordan if a pro-Nasser regime was set up in Amman? This readiness to establish a *casus belli* as a sort of insurance against a possible deterioration in the situation was made easier for the Israelis by their ability to turn these fears into instant military action. Their greater military strength, certainly in the short term, encouraged them to take every immediate advantage. This prevailing orthodoxy was occasionally questioned in Israel, but no change was forthcoming. After one retaliation against Syria, the Left Wing Socialist Party, Mapam, protested in its papers, but its leaders remained in the Coalition cabinet.

Thus, when the temperature in the Middle East did rise, as in 1967, Israel's automatic reaction was to see every political gesture which went unanswered, every manoeuvre which went unchecked, as embodying a decisive threat to her future physical security. The political issues of the area were thus frozen, because any possible change was only interpreted in a strictly military light by Israel. The normally fertile and receptive imagination of the Israelis seemed to have been conditioned by years of frontier skirmishing into accepting the customary military judgement that the problem was essentially a military and not a political one, and that only a military solution could be found.

3

Refugees

how can I use in my paper?

ANYBODY WHO believes that the Balfour Declaration provided the solution to the Jewish problem should remember that its outcome actually gave rise to the problem of an Arab displacement almost as large as the Jewish displacement the whole thing was expected to solve.

In August 1948—half-way through the first Arab–Israel war—the number of Arab refugees was put at 300,000, of which two-thirds were under eighteen, one-third under five, and one in ten were expectant mothers. This figure rose. In October 1948 it was 472,000, in November 600,000, in March 700,000, in April 900,000 and in June 1,000,000. These early figures were probably exaggerated and certainly dropped back when fighting stopped. After the armistice there may have been some extra checking, or it may have been that any reliable census had to wait until the United Nations Relief Organisation was functioning properly. After some years, however, the figures soon returned to that level, with 880,000 being registered in June 1952, 905,000 in 1956, and 922,000 in 1957. The million mark was passed in 1958 with 1,037,000, of which more than half were under sixteen. By 1961 there were 1,125,000 refugees listed.

Who were the refugees? Arabs have a habit of fleeing from situations of uncertainty, turbulence or foreboding, and of returning when peace is restored or when word reaches them that their fears were unfounded. It has happened over and over again in the Arab world. (Christ, incidentally, started his life as a refugee.) Recently in Aden the population was halved overnight by the terrorism and the prospects of a violent civil war when the British left. The exodus was not only of Somalis and Yemenis—expatriates in that case—but of local people too. In Palestine itself, 40,000 Arabs fled during the Arab rebellion of 1936–1939. But they came back when peace was restored.

It is probably something rather difficult for Europeans to

understand, since in cases where European refugees have been created, the victims themselves have probably waited until the last moment before fleeing, and accepted the finality of their flight in a way seldom accepted by refugees in the Middle East. It is therefore easier there for people to leave their homes and stay away with friends or relatives, carrying most of their belongings with them. Europeans might flinch from refugee status because of the impossibility or impracticability of taking all their possessions with them. In the Middle East, few potential refugees probably possess enough chattels to hinder their flight. What is important to them is more often the plot of land which they have to leave behind.

It is certainly true that many Arabs would have temporarily fled from places of particular contention during the 1948 war. There were atrocities and rumours of atrocities on both sides to speed them on. Both sides indulged in atrocity propaganda, just as both sides indulged in atrocities. Perhaps the main difference between their propaganda, however, and one which can be similarly ascribed in almost every field of Arab-Israeli propaganda during the last twenty years, was that the Arab population to whom their propaganda was directed was a less critical, more gullible, and more simple audience than the Jews. They were taught to hate the Jews, but their belief that the Jews possessed the very characteristics which they were taught to hate only helped to increase their terror, and persuaded them to flee before what they had every reason to believe must be a great wrath to come.

It is true that both sides at first used force to expel or contain their people in certain areas. But afterwards there was a massive Arab exodus which has always been said by Israelis to have been a planned manoeuvre, officially encouraged by the Arabs. In fact there has never been any evidence of official Arab encouragement of their people to leave their homes. It may also be significant to recall that in the middle of the war Ben Gurion said that situation would be settled by military power alone, and that any repatriation of the Arabs would be 'folly'.

At the time of the Rhodes armistice talks early in 1949 it

became clear that the Israeli Government did not envisage any solution to the refugee problem which involved the Arabs' repatriation to Israeli territory. They believed strongly that minority problems were best solved by population transfer. Moreover, for the first time they said that the former Arab areas in Israel were now full to capacity with Jewish immigrants from Europe, and that it would not be possible therefore to reabsorb the Arabs. This argument was, of course, vitiated by the Israelis themselves when they proved over the next fifteen years how much greater the absorptive capacity in Israel was than was then claimed.

This improvement was undoubtedly made possible by the frugality of the Israelis' approach to land, their superb achievement in reclamation, and their gifted husbandry, and one can say almost certainly that any given acreage in the Middle East can absorb more Jews than it can Arabs. But the point was not lost on the Arabs that, while there was not the reabsorptive capacity for Arab refugees to return to Israel, there seemed adequate capacity for Jewish refugees from Europe to return, and indeed the underlying principle with the 'Law of Return' in Israel was that the country had to extend its hospitality and citizenship to each and every Jew who returned. And there were 12,000,000 Jews. The improbability of many of them returning was an actuarial calculation which did nothing to dent the Arabs' distaste for this apparent contradiction between the available territory and the number of people who might want to fill it. There were too many people to fill it already.

Israel offered instead to assist in the resettlement of the Arabs elsewhere, and also offered to pay compensation for Arab property destroyed or requisitioned during the war. The compensation would at first be offset by deductions arising out of charges incurred by Arab damage to Jewish property in the war.

The Arabs would have none of it. In July 1949, the Israeli Government offered to repatriate wives, unmarried daughters and sons under fifteen years old, which in all would have amounted to about 100,000 people. They wanted the refugee problem, however, to be negotiated only in the context of a general peace settlement, whereas the Arabs later returned to their point that it should be done in isolation. They clung tenaciously to a United Nations resolution of 1948 (December) which said that those wishing to return to their homes should be allowed to do so. That resolution still stands, is still not being implemented, and in spite of its good intentions it has in a way been innocently as responsible for the deterioration in the refugee situation as all the other factors over the years.

Fortified by the apparent international success which accompanied the resolution, and the belief that they could command more than the world's moral support, the Arabs placed themselves in a position over the refugee problem where they could not afford to do or say anything that implied a dilution of the pure and uncomplicated sentiments of this resolution. There was no attempt to plan against the possibility that the resolution would not be implemented. They refused to see that this declaration of moral support was about as far as the international community would be prepared to go, and that on its own it was not adequate to change the Israeli policy. The Arabs believed that the existence or admission of such planning would automatically weaken the force of their case against Israel by the admission that there was some kind of qualified alternative.

When, in December 1949, the UN sponsored an economic survey of the refugee problem which recommended that work should be created for them in their refugee areas, involving drainage schemes and the establishment of some elementary horticultural industry—more to create work as therapy than as an economic undertaking—the whole scheme was viewed with suspicion by the Arabs. They regarded any help of this kind as betraying a wish on the part of the West just to bury the refugee problem under viable alternative courses of action and then proclaim that there was no problem.

Later on, in 1952, another UN sponsored scheme called for the provision of 250 million dollars from voluntary contributions from UN members on the assumption that if these voluntary contributions could be found the host governments (Arab) would also put up some money and the whole plight of the refugees could be improved in the context of a general three-year economic development programme for the area. This was again objected to by the Arabs, not only on the grounds that it was not solving the essential moral and political problem of refugees, which could only be done by Israel accepting the principle of responsibility, but also on the grounds that the UN scheme, was an infringement of their economic sovereignty. So none of these schemes was adopted.

Meanwhile on the ground the position of refugees had sunk into a kind of torpor of subsistence. A whole host of apparently insurmountable difficulties were raised during the early months. There were food difficulties, aggravated not only by the sheer distributional problem of ensuring that each and every refugee received his ration, while nobody got two, but as much by the dietary difficulties involved in keeping the Arabs alive on a very limited budget and small amount of daily calories. The diet had to fit in not only with the health necessity, but with the eating habits and tastes of the refugees, who could hardly, even in their present predicament, have their tastes ignored to the point of being treated as statistics in a calorie-consumption table.

The refugees were roughly divided into three categories. A small number were wealthy middle class, possibly property owners or small businessmen, who simply wanted to return for a short time to wind up their business and retrieve something of their investments. In October 1952, Israel released £1m. from the blocked accounts of refugees, which was about a quarter of the total sum blocked during the war. It benefited about 2,000 people and another 15,000 refugees were expected to benefit from the remainder being unblocked—about £3m.— in 1954. The second unblocking, incidentally, saw the rare occasion of direct negotiations between the General Refugees' Congress of Palestine and the Government of Israel.

The great mass of refugees were the peasants anxious to return to their homes, probably not for high-sounding historical reasons but from the inalienable attachment to one's own plot of land, which is an inherent trait of people living at a subsistence level. There are some arguments that if they are at a subsistence level anyway it makes no difference where they subsist. Conversely, however, probably the main, if not the only, reason why their subsistence is tolerable and not misery is because of the familiarity of their surroundings. This is something they could never admit, but which, incidentally, would probably persuade many of the new generation now not to leave their present surroundings and move back, were it not for the propaganda and the biased education which they have received.

Finally there was the nationalist element among the refugees. It has always been the presence of nationalists which has governed the Israeli arguments against repatriation of the Arabs, on the grounds that Israel's security could not be jeopardised by absorbing into her population people who are dedicated to overthrowing the state. In fact the United Nations resolution allowed Israel to control the repatriation within the interests of her security, presumably by screening applicants beforehand, but the Israel reply to that is normally that all Arab refugees would present a security risk. This is obviously not true, although it is probably fair to say that it may be less untrue now than it was twenty years ago when the refugee problem was first created. The years of propaganda and slanted education which the refugee children have received make it likely that the younger generation are probably more indoctrinated with pan-Arabism and anti-Israelism than their parents were, in spite of the fact that the young have never set foot in the territories from which their parents fled.

On the other hand it is difficult to see what other aspirations a young refugee can have. Faced with the obvious exclusion of the refugees from Israel, faced with the obvious incapacity of the Arab world as at present constituted to do anything about the Israel problem, a young Palestinian can have little alternative but to look to the day when the Arab world becomes sufficiently united to make its weight felt against Israel. The frustrations which must attend such aspirations in great measure explain the subversive, disappointed and uncompromising attitudes normally expressed by the Palestinian leadership.

By the time of the 1949 armistice agreements, when the refugees were said to number 900,000, they were divided up as between 425,000 on the West Bank of Jordan, 225,000 in Gaza, 130,000 in Lebanon, 85,000 in Syria, 11,000 in Egypt and 4,000 in Iraq. These concentrations became more dispersed as Pales-

43

tinians sought their fortunes further afield in the Arab world, and today you will find Palestinians occupying senior administrative, legal or government posts all over the Arab world, and particularly in the Gulf states. Many more work in the oil fields of the Gulf, yet even they normally retain their link with the old refugee apparatus in the old camps, either by leaving their families there or sending remittances from their wages.

Their fear of being assimilated into non-Palestinian countries still seems to act as a powerful enough barrier to stop them forfeiting completely the refugee status because, as it turned out, the material advantages of remaining a refugee probably came to outweigh the advantages of making a completely new life in a new country. Besides, the irrevocable nature of such a decision—there was no going back on it, no further registration of refugees—is not something to appeal to the average Arab mentality, which flinches from categorical decisions either way.

This sort of choice was a long way off from those early days, however, before even Jordan extended her citizenship to the refugees, which followed on the formal annexation of the West Bank in 1950. At the start the situation was terrible. Many of them were poorly clothed, badly housed, crowded into the available huts—or tents in the case of Gaza. Thousands of them were idle and unqualified, more than half were illiterate. A few managed to find occupation in tailoring, and service trades of that kind, but for the mass of them there was nothing to do. Nevertheless, in spite of these physically daunting disadvantages, and the severe winters on the Jordanian hills, the early fears that the death rate would soar through epidemics were unfounded. Only in the tuberculosis rate and the prevalence of bronchial and respiratory troubles were the refugees to provide above-average illness ratings, as well as the particularly infectious dysentery and eye infections which were prevalent in the area.

In 1952 Israel offered her Arab refugees full citizenship. Of course this act of integrating her own Arab refugees has shown that she was fully facing up to the consequences of their presence —something that only Jordan had fully done among the Arab states. Egypt studiously kept her refugees separate, and indeed they were not allowed to leave Gaza in favour of metropolitan

44

Egypt on the west side of the Suez Canal. On the other hand, Israel, in a way, also accepted a philosophical disadvantage in integrating her own Arabs because in doing so she accepted the principle of a non-Jewish population within Israel and this diluted her absolute earlier position that the only new Israel citizens were to be Jews. The Arabs never took the argument against Israel this far, perhaps because they never accepted that Israel's Arab population was fully integrated.

The basic difficulty for the international world dealing with the problem is that outsiders, unlike the Arabs, cannot avoid seeing it primarily as a problem of humanity. The plight of the refugees is really on the ground, and one would have thought it would have evoked all the sympathy and urgency to produce a remedy that was needed. Yet to the Arabs it is a burning political issue and the almost metaphysical nature of their complaint— the abstract quality of the *politics* of the refugee problem— arouses much fiercer indignation than their actual privation, perhaps because man for man they may be actually physically and materially better off than many of the people in the countries to which they are affiliated. The other Arabs could hardly agitate against their material condition when it compares not unfavourably with the rest of the Arab world. This may explain the Arabs' reluctance to allow any measure of material alleviation to be confused with the politics of the question.

For instance, the refugees, half of whom were born since the 1948 war, are on the whole probably better educated than the Arab populations around them. There are more than 200 UNRWA schools, and in the absence of any repatriation the time is bound to come when their sole identification with the old areas within Israel stems from the teaching they receive rather than any actually remembered link with the land in question. In a sense this could be an even more dangerous proposition because the world is coming to learn that there is nothing so subversive as an education programme which outpaces the necessary economic development to go with it. Educated, unemployed or unsatisfied people are infinitely more combustible than uneducated ones, and the primitive wish of the old refugee peasants to be returned to their land has now almost been replaced by a fanaticism, an

45

intellectual quality which is as hard to dislodge, and twice as violent if unsatisfied.

For some years now the other Arab countries seem to have realised the dangers to them also of an unsettled refugee population. The frustrations were continually fanned by the Arab propaganda machine, but without any outlet there was no certainty that they would not turn on their own. In 1964 the Palestine Liberation Organisation was formed to give some release for their energies and aspirations, but the refusal by Egypt to assimilate the refugees was as much motivated by their fear of the effect of a large influx of disgruntled Palestinians on the general body politic of Egypt as by the philosophical reasons for continuing to observe their Palestinianism. Jordan's assimilation may have been unavoidable, but it has often led to a situation where the Palestinian tail wags the Transjordan dog, and most of King Hussein's energies have had to be directed to coping with this condition.

Another interesting aspect of the Arab nation's approach to the refugees has been their attitude to the enormous financial problem posed by the refugees. Needless to say, the UN programme is continually subjected to economic pressure and there has been a constant drive to cut the ration lists. Any listed refugee who earned more than £15 a month was taken off the ration list, with the result that job-hunting outside the camps was not pursued with tremendous zeal. Once off the lists it was almost impossible to get reinstated as a refugee, and yet, of course, it was not so hard to lose one's job.

This all encouraged a great reluctance to sacrifice refugee status except in exchange for cast-iron career prospects, which were unlikely to be forthcoming in most of the volatile economic conditions of the Middle East. Significantly, the main place where refugees have finally decided to take the plunge is in Kuwait and the other oil regions in the Gulf, where job transfers appear to have happened simultaneously, without planning, because presumably the economic prospects on the oil coast are just about as good as one could expect.

Apart from this unplanned transfer what specific assistance did the Arabs give to the refugees? The answer is very little.

They had always tended to see the UN Relief Organisation as an agency more ready to condone the refugee situation than to solve it. Economic pressure was forcing the UN to be careful with their finances and they periodically had to reduce their facilities to the provision of basic needs for the refugees, such as food, clothing and housing, while dispensing with the frills on the programme such as vocational training and rehabilitation schemes. At first this seemed to be in the Arabs' interests, in that it accorded with the political view that nothing should be done to conceal the unacceptable position of the refugees, and significantly only Saudi Arabia, of all the Arab states, contributed any funds to the relief organisation, and her contribution was not much.

Egypt made facilities available at Port Said for the shipment of supplies which the Egyptians claimed represented 350,000 dollars a year. Jordan paid for the camp maintenance, but not the camps. Syria paid for medical services and the Lebanon waived the rents on the headquarters building of the relief organisation. Apart from a Yugoslavian contribution of 40,000 dollars in 1947 there was no communist contribution. But by 1957 there were signs that the Arab governments themselves realised a little the danger of inciting dissatisfaction to actual physical breaking point, and in September of that year Jordan, Lebanon, Sudan, Morocco and Saudi Arabia all contributed small sums to the fund.

Where then has the money come from to keep the million refugees alive ? For the answer one has to look to those self-same imperialists who attract so much of the blame in the Middle East. To be fair to them, if they are to blame they are certainly paying for it. That would certainly appear to be the Arab and Israeli attitude to the question of subsistence for the refugees. 'It is not our problem, let somebody else pay.' In doing so they both show themselves blinded by the politics of the question into forgetting that a refugee is, or should be in human terms, the problem of everybody who is not one. Since the start of the refugees' initial fund until the summer 1967 the United States had channelled into it about 330m. dollars, Great Britain 100m. dollars, and France 12m. dollars. The contribution of the rest of the world can be gauged by the fact that these sums represent about 95 per cent of the total.

Now since 1967 a kind of second tier of refugees has been created by those refugees who fled in their thousands across the Jordan before the Israel advance and capture of that river's West Bank. But publicity towards their plight since the war, severe though it is, has tended to overlook the fact that at least 750,000 refugees who remained are now under Israeli control. The problem beforehand was an external one for Israel, and she could remain insulated from all aspects of it except the political. Now, and for as long as she remains in control of the Gaza strip and the West Bank of the Jordan, the refugee question is an internal issue, with all the physical problems of administration, finance, security and immigration firmly on Israel's doorstep.

It would be sad if a new post-war settlement between Israel and the Arabs was reached simply on terms dictated by Israel's demand for geographical security, because that would leave out the refugee problem altogether. And yet what sort of solution for them is there? My suggestions for the possible ingredients of an eventual settlement between Israel and the Arabs will be dealt with in a later chapter. But there are one or two principles which have consistently applied to the refugee question over the last twenty years, and continue to do so now, in spite of the changes of 1967.

Any final solution to the problem must pay more than lip service to the principle of choice for the refugees—choice between repatriation and rehabilitation. Of course, Israel's requirements over security would have to be met, but Israel has never actually accepted that the refugees have the right of choice, even allowing for Israel's sovereign right to vet applications and veto them on security grounds if necessary. Israel has often said she would willingly assist in the rehabilitation of refugees elsewhere, but it is the refusal even to consider the *principle* of repatriation which has so inflamed the Arab world. It would be unrealistic, however, to imagine that any solution, even allowing for the free choice of refugees between these alternatives, would or should involve a large-scale physical transfer of populations from their present locations to former territories inside Israel. Apart from the fact that these territories are now occupied, apart from the fact that no Israel Government which allowed such a thing would survive within Israel, most observers believe that once the honours had been done, most refugees would opt for rehabilitation elsewhere, provided they were fully assimilated, rather than opt for a return to living in Israel within the jurisdiction of an Israeli Government. A very convincing testimony to the likelihood of this happening can be found in the numbers of refugees who have voted with their feet in exactly that manner since the ending of the 1967 war.

Although Israel has been reluctant to accept back into occupied territory even those refugees who fled, some 14,000 have in fact returned—about one in ten of those who fled. But what is more significant is that in the same period another 100,000-odd have left the occupied areas, not in a wave but in a continuous trickle day after day, week after week, expressing their preference for a new refugee status somewhere else, but at least under an Arab sun. The remainder are refugees from what is now Israeli territory, however, and it is no good Israel claiming that she has taken in many Jewish refugees from other Arab countries and therefore has already redressed the balance. Among the many other facets of the Arab-Israeli argument, the refugee question stands out as the area where Israel could have afforded to adopt a more flexible approach whatever the Arabs themselves did, and that is something Israel has so far failed to do.

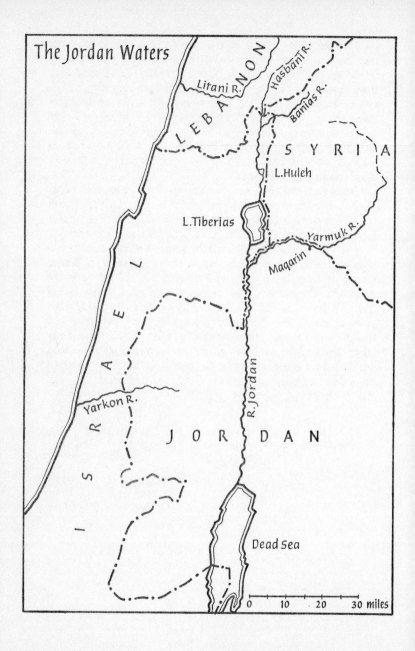

The Jordan Waters

Litani R.

LEBANON

Hasbani R.

Banias R.

S Y R I A

L. Huleh

L. Tiberias

Yarmuk R.

Maqarin

I S R A E L

Yarkon R.

J O R D A N

R. Jordan

Dead Sea

0   10   20   30 miles

4

Jordan Waters

Four countries—Syria, Jordan, Lebanon and Israel, share the River Jordan. It rises in one, its main tributary is in another, and the third possesses many miles of one of its banks. The main lake through which it flows is bordered by Israel and Syria, though effective control of the outlet of that lake belongs to Israel.

The rights and responsibilities of littoral states in a situation like this have grown up by international code and convention over many years and through many difficulties, but there must have been few situations as difficult to resolve as this one. Water in the Middle East is anyway at a premium. In the case of the Jordan, this scarcity and consequent value has an additional price placed upon it in the form of the unrelenting political hostility between two of the littoral states and the third, which has made the possibility of co-operation over water resources that much more difficult, if not absolutely unattainable.

The Jordan flows from north to south in the Great Rift Valley, which actually stretches on down through the Gulf of Aqaba, the Red Sea and into East Africa. The river itself ends in the Dead Sea. From source to end its total length is about seventy miles, more than two-thirds of which are below sea level. Its two main sources are at Dan and Banias and unite below sea level just inside Israel. From there it drops 680 feet in the next nine miles into a delta which opens into the Sea of Galilee (Lake Tiberias). South of the Sea of Galilee the river receives its main tributary, the Yarmuk, which flows in from the east, and various other salt springs rise in the valley as it descends to the Dead Sea, 1,300 feet below sea level.

The high ground to the West of the Jordan lies in the rain shadow of the escarpment to the east and the average annual rainfall on the high ground is about four inches, ten times the level on the river bed and nearly double that which obtains to the east. Further south the rainfall is unpredictable but seldom more than eight inches a year.

The flow is intermittent. During the rainy season of January and February the Jordan overflows its banks, flooding the depression which lies on either side of the actual river bed, and making it fertile after the flood level falls. During the season of rain and melting snow the temperature can often drop almost to freezing. In the summer the heat is sometimes 110 in the shade Most of the tributaries are wadis which are dry except after the rains, and the main aim in irrigation is to capture the water and siphon it off before it is lost.

Throughout its history the Jordan has proved a natural frontier of a kind. It provided the border of the Promised Land into which the Jews were originally led and it always roughly divided the settled from the nomadic populations. In the past there was little settlement actually within the Jordan Valley itself, with the exception of Jericho which was anyway raised up slightly from the low point at the river bed.

Local peasants were accustomed to use the valley in the winter for pasture and small cultivation, and to retire on the approach of summer. The river was not greatly important because the water was not stored; and because nobody lived there, little trouble was taken to irrigate the immediate area next to the river banks, which were flooded. One can see that Jordan's water was not vital for the farmers on the high ground at either side of the Rift Valley, which had a reasonable rainfall. But it could be important either in the immediate area of the river—which had not been populated permanently—or elsewhere in the littoral countries which border on the river.

This point really lies at the root of the problem of the Jordan river. Should the countries which share the river bank be able to transfer the water by irrigation schemes to areas far removed from the river itself? Was their entitlement to use the water absolute, or only relative to the bank area and its immediate hinterland? The other question is what proportion of the available water at any given point in the river should be siphoned off? Should it be worked out on a basis of the length of bank owned, or should the countries at the higher end of the river, who obviously have more power over the water supply even if they have less water, be obliged to honour the needs of the other littoral states further downstream?

The fairest ruling on this problem seems to have come from a report of technicians from the United States who surveyed the area from a purely technical point of view. Their technical judgement ignored the political overtones of the water problem there, but in doing so they probably came closer to the correct position than any other formula. They said that the water in the catchment area, such as the Jordan Valley, should not be diverted outside that area unless the requirements of all those who use, or genuinely intend to use, the water within the area have been satisfied.

The question running through the Jordan waters argument between the Arabs and Israel has centred on the right of Israel to divert Jordan water for use outside the immediate Jordan area, and conversely the right of the source countries to retaliate by denying Israel any water, or more than a very little, by a diversion of the mainstream to keep its early passage out of Israeli territory. The tragedy is that the outcome of the dispute has resulted in the area as a whole receiving less water. There are many who have assumed that the only solution will come when water is no longer at such a premium in the area, and when desalination and other sources of power have managed to defuse the problem of water for an equitable distribution of the Jordan to be arranged.

How did it all start? The first scheme for a more scientific approach to Jordan water seems to have been the Rutenberg Scheme of 1921 which involved damming the southern end of the Sea of Galilee to make it a storage reservoir for power. An irrigation canal would have been built down the West Bank of the Jordan and a second power station built further up the river at Huleh, where the marshes would be drained to allow another 5,000 acres of land for cultivation. The scheme was to catch the rains, which fell for only four months, and enlarge the storage capacity of the Sea of Galilee, which was anyway a natural reservoir.

Under the Mandate the scheme—although prepared by Zionists —went through and started operating in 1932. During its construction, companies of Jewish workers had worked on the project in Transjordan during the 1930s but no action was taken against them.

After the war the situation showed little change from that in operation in the early 1930s. It was then that the basic conflict emerged. The exodus of refugees from Israel—conquered territory in old Palestine meant that for the first time there was a settled population in the Jordan Valley. That is where they came to rest, and if the area had not been settled much in the past, because other places were preferable, the shortage of alternative choices to the refugees meant that they had to make do with what came their way. The area provided an uncomfortable, though not irretrievable prospect, but their only hope of making it at all palatable was to irrigate the potentially fertile valley and cultivate it, so that they could alleviate their economic distress and make it a more amenable environment in which to live. This meant they required Jordan's water for that area.

Israel, on the other hand, also had a problem of a new settlement in potentially barren country. The influx of new Jewish immigrants could only be borne by the settlement in areas not formerly populated, or cultivated, and the Jewish reclamation of desert areas was a formidable achievement, showing an application for husbandry which possibly startled the immigrants themselves, mostly coming as they did from urban communities in Europe. But for this work they needed as much water as the Arabs. There was obviously not enough water for all these extra projects, however, particularly when one added the existing areas which had always relied on water from the Jordan in the first place.

This problem was no doubt exaggerated by the fact that it was not just an isolated scrap over who needed most water. The reasons for wanting the water were a highly inflammable political issue on their own, directly involving the question of Arab refugees on the one hand and the Jewish immigration into Israel on the other. Thus they tended to treat the question as a political issue, whereas without those overtones the littoral powers could, and probably would, have to come to an understanding in the normal manner of littoral states, even when hard economic interests come between them.

The first shooting incident arising out of the Jordan water diversion occurred in April 1951. The Israelis had a scheme for diverting surplus Jordan water from the Huleh marshes in the north across Galilee by pipeline to irrigate their new settlement areas in the northern part of the Negev Desert. The shooting probably started because the Israeli pipeline work and the draining of the marshes involved an area which had been formally demilitarised after the 1948 war. The Israeli work also involved the transfer of Arab peasants who lived in the demilitarised zone to other areas in Israel. The Syrians claimed that this act prejudiced the ceasefire agreement and the UN agreed, so that eventually Israel agreed to cease that part of the work which would have affected the resident Arab peasants until an overall agreement had been reached. But Israeli work continued elsewhere in the demilitarised zone, with only temporary stoppages.

By this time, any hopes there were of persuading the countries to co-operate over the mutual water supply were already slim. The original plan for the area, based on surveys made during the 1930s by the Transjordan Government, was exhumed after the 1939 war by King Abdullah. The intention was to irrigate a great acreage in the Jordan Valley between the Sea of Galilee and the Dead Sea by making the Sea of Galilee into a storage reservoir so as not to squander the winter floods. It also meant diverting the Yarmuk river into the Sea of Galilee, and the scheme, if successful, contained good prospects for developing the Jordan Valley as a fertile, well irrigated, tropical and subtropical area with possibilities for vegetables and stone fruits. Most of the water—about seven-eighths—would have gone to Jordan and the rest to Israel.

With the influx of refugees into the Jordan Valley in 1947 and 1948 this question became acute and urgent. Whereas before it had occupied developers, thinking in the long term, it was now of great immediacy and of great political moment too. The absurd, though tragic, aspect of the situation was that either side, either

Israel or Jordan, could on its own appropriate large amounts of water—Israel at the Huleh marshes, or Jordan by diverting the Yarmuk, which was one main tributary. But if they took the water independently of each other they could only use about half the water available because the other half could only be saved and stored if the Sea of Galilee were used as a storage reservoir, and this could only be done by mutual consent. The Jews controlled the Sea of Galilee but the Jordanians controlled the Yarmuk. By 1951 the imperatives of this situation seemed to have been successfully ignored on both sides, and they prepared to go their separate ways. Three years later, however, a last attempt was made to stimulate both sides into treating the problem as a regional water problem which must transcend their national attitudes if it was to succeed.

Three separate new water plans were then published, one Arab, one Israeli and one American. The American-sponsored report was prepared by a body of technicians solely concerned with the possibilities of development of the area from the available water base. It was thus a non-political engineering study. It proposed an increase in the storage capacity of the Sea of Galilee by more than two-thirds and also the building of another smaller reservoir in Jordanian territory over the Yarmuk at Maqarin. This would then increase the available water. However, it would not alter the actual proportionate distribution which still awarded the lion's share to Jordan. It just meant that by mutual co-operation—that is to say between Jordan, Israel and Syria—they would all have got more water than before.

The report of the technical committee of the Arab League had different findings, but contained one political concession of absolutely fundamental importance—recognition of Israel's right to have water from the Jordan. In the distribution Israel was not to receive such a generous share as she would have under the American scheme, but after Jordan she would have received more water than the other two states. Basically, the ratios were 67 to 33 Arab over Israel in the American report and 80 to 20 in the Arab report. This must be set against the fact that of the annual flow of water out of the Jordan water-shed 77% originates in Arab territory and only 25% in Israel.

Apart from that difference in proportions, the Arabs objected to the American scheme because it was based on the increased use of the Sea of Galilee as a reservoir. They said that it would leave them at the mercy of Israel for their water. They bolstered this political argument with a technical one that they would lose more water from evaporation in the Sea of Galilee—owing to its greater salinity—than they would by building a smaller reservoir on the Yarmuk, safely on Jordanian territory and under Jordanian control. Israel, they said, would be allowed to draw her irrigation waters from a canal flowing south from this, and her agreed share of the waters above the Sea of Galilee. Both plans foresaw the use of electric power plants.

The Israeli plan was very different, and would have involved more than twice the expense over a period of twenty-five years, but it also called for the integration into the scheme of the surplus waters of the Lebanese river, the Litani.

The Israeli arguments against the other schemes were that by ignoring the Litani they were not truly regional, that no account was taken of political realities, and that the irrigation of the Negev Desert was either deliberately ignored or excluded. The first and last of these reasons were strongly connected, since it was under a regional approach to the development of Jordan's water that Israel justified or defended her transfer of it away from the valley, over the watershed and down to the Desert. The inclusion of the Litani would have benefited Israel considerably. This would have offset the fact, strongly suspected in Israel, that in any regional share-out of just the Jordan alone she was bound to get a smaller share than she wanted and certainly than she needed for irrigation outside the immediate catchment area.

It must obviously have been tempting to Israel to put up with the water penalties and go along with the Arab League scheme in exchange for the considerable victory of reaching an agreement with the Arabs which not only acknowledged her existence but actually acknowledged her rights as a sovereign member of the region, ranking second among the littoral states of the Jordan. The talks went on for about two years while the American mediator made extensive modifications to the American report so that it eventually closely resembled the original Arab proposals. Still, the prospects of an agreement lured Israel, although she was apprehensive about any arrangement within the plan for an international authority to regulate the use of water from the Sea of Galilee, since this might constitute an infringement of her sovereignty.

Nevertheless, by 1956 Israel and Jordan were ready to sign an agreement. This stipulated Jordan's primary right to the water, but underlined also Israel's insistence on her right to convey the water to any site chosen in Israel, and not necessarily ones in the catchment area. Agreement was never reached, most probably because the political explosions and eruptions of 1956 and the continued Syrian hostility to any agreement finally put paid to its chances. The parties finally went their own ways.

Jordan decided to go ahead with her diversion of the Yarmuk and Israel continued with the work at Huleh on the Syrian frontier which had been held up in case there was to be an acceptance of the overall scheme. This was the scheme which first caused trouble back in 1951 and had been a recurring source of Syrian-Israeli discontent since then. The Israelis had in fact never pushed it to the point of a showdown with Syria because they had calculated that during the period from 1953–1960 agricultural expansion planned would have been adequately provided with water by the existing flows from the Yarkon and Kishon, two minor rivers within Israel national boundaries. Israel actually gave an assurance that her independent plans would never involve drawing more than that amount to which she was entitled under the original American scheme (called the 'Johnson Scheme' after the American mediator). However, this ignored the fact that the total amount of water available all round was less than it would have been if the littoral states had jointly developed the water resources. Israel would have been more correct to say that she would not draw more than the *percentage* awarded to her under the Johnson entitlement, which would have brought her less water but possibly more tolerance from the Arabs.

They gradually reacted in an increasingly hostile manner to Israel's policy. In 1960 Jordan proposed that Israel's plans should be baulked by depriving her of most of the head waters of the Jordan on which she relied. This could be done by diverting the two rivers which were the sources of the Jordan—the Hasbani to the Litani and the Banias to the Yarmuk. Questions of actual defence crept back into the issue, aggravated no doubt by the fact that there was a drought, which was having a serious effect on crops for the third year running.

Between them these two rivers supply about 40% of the water which flows into Lake Tiberias, and most of which Israel was entitled to under the schemes. In fact the scheme was going to involve the Arabs in great construction work and expenditure to ensure that the water was first of all captured and then taken away for use elsewhere because it could not be absorbed locally. Unless these conditions were fulfilled, at immense cost and no mean engineering achievement, the water would simply escape and flow back down the watershed. That is what the Israelis felt, but to make certain they periodically delayed the programmes with artillery fire and bombing raids, and by spring 1967 they were confident they had delayed the programme for at least twenty years at the current pace of work on it.

The campaign of 1967 transformed this situation, however, in that Israel captured all the key points at issue in the water dispute. As long as Israel remains in occupation of the present territory she conquered in the 1967 war, there is no water problem, because neither Jordan nor Syria has control over any of the areas necessary to reinforce their arguments. This must be, for Israel, a potent argument for staying in those areas.

At the time of writing, Israel is still in possession of all the relevant areas, and no settlement is in sight. There have, since the 1967 war, been various plans put forward for a joint approach to the question of desalination, involving internationally financed schemes of research, development, and the construction of nuclear power stations in Israel and Jordan. There is also, of course, pressure in Israel to remain in possession, thus obviating the necessity for securing an agreement with the Arabs on the water question, since they would have no alternative but to accept the *force majeure*. Either way, it is still quite obvious that the water problem of the area cannot now be divorced from the general political questions affecting a settlement. Sad though this is, in terms of the development projects for the Jordan Valley, it is clear that no scheme will get passed purely on its technical merits alone. Power politics will decide the issue.

5

Arab Nationalism and Israel

ALTHOUGH THE Arabs as a whole suffered Ottoman domination reluctantly, their opposition to it was seldom coherent and certainly nothing resembling an Arab nationalist front was formed during those centuries. Arab nationalism probably finds its source in the introduction of western ideas into the Middle East after Napoleon's invasion of Egypt. Throughout its history, however, there had been the contradiction, or at least the conflict, between nationalism and pan-Arabism. Nationalism was a product of Egyptian thought and reflected that Egypt more than any other area under Ottoman domination had a definite national identity which was hard to find anywhere else in the Middle East. Pan-Arabism came much more from Syria, where intellectuals, having no real nation, had to crystallise their frustrations and aspirations in something more philosophical than nationalism.

With the improvement in communications in the twentieth century pan-Arabism became at least a common idea, Arabic as spoken by Cairo radio a common tongue, and the combination has had the automatic effect of keeping the area bubbling with the traffic of confusing and conflicting streams of political thought. It has also given the Arab world an artificial appearance of unity, which has made the actual moments of testing that unity all the more painful. Arab unity is an idea that has been much preached, but never successfully practised.

The conflict between Arab nationalism and Israel started as an indirect one. The basic enemy of Arab nationalism had been Western imperialism—primarily British but also French and American. More often than not, the enmity shown to Israel has arisen because Israel is seen to be an extension of the imperialist policies of these countries by other means, and no amount of Israeli nationalism has been able to eradicate this association of ideas. To be fair, it is not only the existence of tremendous funds which pour into Israel from the subscriptions of world Jewry which inflame this belief. The Arabs have it from Theodore Herzl, himself, the first organiser of the Zionist movement, who made no secret of his belief that Zionism was essentially colonialism, and that it should therefore be underwritten by Britain and launched from Britain because Britain understood the principles of colonialism better than any country in the world.

In 1890 this may have been a great compliment, but it is of doubtful value today, when the colonial idea is so unfashionable. Indeed, Herzl went even further and looked forward to the day when British strategic interests would favour the establishment of a colonial regime in Palestine. Writing in his diary of 1897 he said, 'I believe it would be a good idea for our cause if the English were forced to leave Egypt. They would be obliged to seek out another road to India in place of the Suez Canal which would then be lost to them or at least rendered insecure. In that event a modern Jewish-Palestine—with a railroad from Jaffa to the Persian Gulf—would resolve their difficulty'.*

It was also an acknowledged strategy in the 1920s during the Mandate, so why should not the Arabs think that in spite of independence Israel continued to exist in the Western interest?

Later, in 1901, Herzl said to a meeting of the English Zionist Federation, 'England with her possessions in Asia should be most interested in Zionism, for the shortest road to India is by way of Palestine. England's great politicians were the first to recognise the need for colonial expansion. That is why Great Britain's ensign flies on all the oceans. And so I must believe that here in England the idea of Zionism, which is a colonial idea, should be easily and quickly understood in its true and most modern form.'

In their moments of darkest suspicion about Western intentions the Arabs had only to look to Herzl for the confirmation of all their fears, however unfounded in reality they might have been.

Although the force of Arab nationalism has often been artificially stimulated to unite the Arab world, or at least to paper over the cracks of crumbling domestic politics, the movement

*Theodore Herzl: *The Diaries of Theodore Herzl*, Gollancz 1958.

nevertheless has its source in a great historical tradition. When periodically the Arabs have become particularly frustrated, or have felt that their long standing feud with Western imperialism still holds out no real hope for their eventual victory, they have turned on Israel.

What is certainly true is that Britain dominated the Arab world for about seventy years, starting with the governorship of Egypt. In the 1920s Lord Curzon, the British Foreign Secretary, was saying that any interference in the affairs of Egypt by another power would be regarded by Britain as an unfriendly act. Britain wanted undisputed control in the area, and by and large achieved this by inserting self-perpetuating clauses in the defence treaties which she set up in the area. Ultimately, twenty years later, when the dispute with Israel reached its peak, it was those same defence treaties which the Arabs came to loathe, because they saw them as the instruments which Britain used to restrain their hostility to Zionism, to hold them back, and thus advance the cause of Zionism.

In fact, when it came to commanding an audience in the West, and particularly Britain, the Arabs normally felt at a disadvantage to the Zionists. They had their apologists, for sure, but the Arabs themselves usually destroyed the rational part of their case by overstatement, and sympathisers with the Arab cause would anyway find it hard to keep their brief tuned to the erratic, emotional and irrational turns in Arab diplomacy. The maddening thing about Arab nationalism is that so much is hyperbole (whether because of the language or the mentality, or a fusion of both, I am not sure) that it tends to spoil the strength of the basic argument and outsiders can be excused for attributing every move, every slogan, to another figment of the Arabs' corporate imagination.

When the Ottoman Empire was carved up at the Lausanne Conference of 1923 various countries emerged—Syria, Iraq, Saudi Arabia, Transjordan and Lebanon. The first and last were under French influence, the others under Britain. Whitehall's policy was to incorporate all Middle East countries into Britain's sphere of influence. When that system failed, or when it became obvious that we could have no direct control over their policies, as a colonial power might have done, Britain then tried to bind them in a series of military alliances.

There was opposition to this in the countries concerned, and Arab nationalism as a force therefore started by opposing the British connection, and the British military presence. There was no link between this opposition and the later antagonism towards Zionism other than the link between suspected British imperialism in both places, sharpened when the implications of the Balfour Declaration came to suggest Jewish statehood rather than merely a Jewish community. This went further when Britain appeared reluctant to grant Palestine independence, like Iraq, and Egypt, which had their independence granted during the 1930s and subsequently also Transjordan in 1946. Why not Palestine? the Arabs asked. Why not grant Palestine independence, and in that case ensure that the part in the Balfour Declaration about the interests of the local population was itself assured by the existence of an Arab regime in Palestine?

Before the Arab rebellion in Palestine in 1936 Arab nationalism was mainly directed against British attempts to preserve her influence intact in the area and underwrite that influence with military alliances. After that date Arabs outside Palestine started to develop an increasing interest in the Palestine problem. This may have been accelerated by the emergence of Egypt as a force in Arab politics after a long period devoted to internal problems. But Egypt and all the other nations still had governments which were bound by the former military agreements with Britain, and this created conditions for the vicious circle which then took over.

The forces of nationalism were against the British imperial connection. The regimes, however, were not powerful enough, against Britain, to do anything about it and indeed in one or two instances Britain showed that her policy included the power and readiness to make or break governments which conflicted with British interests. Thus there was an automatically widening gulf between popular feeling in these countries and the regimes. The Palestine problem aggravated an already uncomfortable situation. Once again popular feeling in the Middle East was pressing

Arab governments to do something about Palestine, while British influence and authority were being exerted to see that the same governments exercised restraint, however much it worked to their domestic disadvantage to do so.

Periodically, Britain bent before the wind of Arab discontent by modifying her policy in the Mandate, or by temporarily bending in the Arabs' favour the policy of 'equal obligation' to Jews and Arabs which had been the original principle in the Mandate. The most notable occasion was the publication of the 1939 White Paper imposing severe limitations on Jewish immigration into Palestine for the next five years. It was brought out because Britain was in the eye of the forthcoming storm in Europe and the British Government realised that they must not push the tolerance of the Arab Governments too far if they also wanted to rely on them in war.

The Arab rulers themselves, caught as they were in this crossfire between their own people urging militancy and the British urging restraint, were able to point to their success over the White Paper as justification of collaborations with Britain. Their argument ran that by collaborating with Britain they were able to have an influence on the Mandate policy which they would not have achieved by resistance. Britain was more likely to listen to her allies than her opponents they said. The danger in this argument was, of course, that when Britain did not listen to them they had nothing else to fall back on.

The Arab defeat by Israel in 1948 was the most terrible let down, as only the collapse of an illusion can be. The illusion was Arab unity. How had the much-vaunted Arab unity managed to be so ineffective?

The truth is that the Arabs were too riven by internal rivalries to make the sort of concerted attack on the infant Israel which might then—but not now—have been successful. The defeat set in motion a profound disillusionment. It was probably one of the immediate causes of the Egyptian revolution in 1952, which led to the rise of President Nasser. Ten years earlier Nasser had already been deeply affected by the revolts in Egypt and Iraq against the British connection. Britain had crushed the one in Iraq, and in Egypt forced King Farouk to change his government to one more friendly to Britain, a gesture which Nasser said Egypt 'accepted on her knees in surrender'.

In 1947 there had been renewed attempts in Iraq to revoke the defence treaty with Britain and some Iraq political parties actually appealed to the Soviet Minister in Baghdad to put Palestine on the Security Council agenda. When the Arab-Israel war broke out Britain observed a total arms embargo, and this definitely inhibited her Arab allies' ability to fight the Israelis—another cause of complaint as Israel meanwhile acquired almost as many arms as she could handle from Czechoslovakia. (It is ironic that when, later, Egypt procured arms from Czechoslovakia this caused a revulsion in the United States where previously opinion had been more favourably disposed to Egypt in her dispute with Britain.)

The Western powers nevertheless continued to search for some kind of Middle East NATO and their policy in the area reflected their belief that they must keep Russia out, although there was no suggestion that they might trade Arab co-operation over the Russian threat for co-operation with them over Israel. The Russian threat at that stage was fairly long-range. Russian pressure in the late 1940s was directed at Turkey and Iran, and the view in London and Washington seemed to be that there was a need for defence in depth against the Soviet threat from central Asia. Governments themselves in the Middle East, notably Iraq and Jordan, agreed with the diagnosis and hastened to form some kind of inner protective screen against the Russian threat. In those days strategic thinking in the cold war still saw the Soviet threat as an overt one, requiring the need for alliances as an overt form of defence. The price these Middle East Governments had to pay for their anti-Soviet protection, however, was to suffer British-induced restrictions on their Israel policies.

In fact what was the Soviet influence at that time ? Communist parties have never been really important in domestic Arab politics—on the rare occasions when they have not been banned altogether. (Israel is the only Middle East country which has an official Communist Party.) But that did not prevent elements in Syria, Iraq and Egypt calling for Soviet assistance, not only over

66

the Israeli question but even advocating an alliance with Russia to balance the British and American power in the area. These calls came from nationalist parties, motivated more by anti-westernism and nationalism than anything like doctrinal communism. The nationalists were primarily anti-western, but to the extent that the alliances could also be criticised for restricting movement on Israel, so they criticised them. The Soviet Union's position thus automatically became an anti-Israeli one since they became synonymous with anti-imperialism in the Middle East. It would have been interesting to see what direction Arab nationalism would have taken either if the Western powers had openly espoused their cause, politically, against Israel or had given them no hostages to imperialism to be used as a stalking horse for their eventual hostility to Israel.

Arab nationalism, after the rise of President Nasser, virtually split into two streams as far as the Arab hostility to Israel was concerned. Those who followed Nasser favoured first an attack on the British position in the Middle East, and only tackling the Israeli position once a genuine Arab independence had been gained. Those who favoured co-operating with the West against Russia in the belief that this would bring some Western co-operation over Israel followed Iraq. Before 1948, in fact, many Egyptians were unhappy at the way King Farouk seemed to drag them into the war with Israel, and President Nasser's first years of power were notable for the moderation shown towards Israel. As a result, there was reasonable quiet on the Israel front during the early fifties. President Nasser even let one or two Israeli ships through the Suez Canal, although all the trappings of belligerence were maintained. The prize courts remained sitting in Egypt, and there was no readiness to regard the armistice agreement as a long-term arrangement.

President Nasser's more immediate objective, however, was to sabotage the proposed Western alliance of the Baghdad Pact, which included Iraq, Turkey, Iran, Pakistan and Britain, with the United States as an associate. This pact took the place of the Middle East Defence Community which British and American policy had unsuccessfully tried to establish. Jordan noticeably kept out of it. President Nasser's attempts were not really finally successful until the overthrow of the Iraq monarchy in 1958, but the destruction of the Baghdad Pact was during that period undoubtedly of more importance to him than the destruction of Israel.

The Western anti-Sovietism in the Middle East was interesting because it, in the end, threatened to defeat its own object. It is true that Russian policy was to penetrate the Middle East and to make life as difficult there as possible for the West—particularly in view of the increasing economic sensitivity of the area as the oil started flowing.

After the war the communists tried subversion, and their recognition of Israel can probably be put down to twin influences: firstly, because they saw it as an anti-British force because of the terrorism of the past years—and therefore anti-colonial—and secondly, because of its divisive effect on the already volatile politics of the area. But their attempts at communist subversion in the area were largely unsuccessful. The social and industrial structure in Middle East countries was just not suitable for that brand of communism. Besides, there were no unions, and still are not. They found that Arab nationalism was essentially a bourgeois movement not a communist one, and it still is. They found eventually, much later, that the contradictions of Arab socialism and Arab nationalism made it very hard to find any common ground except Israel, and that is why hostility to Israel has become the common denominator of Soviet contacts with the Middle East, because they know they will not go wrong.

Russia's position in the Arab world was helped by the Suez affair. In the Eisenhower doctrine, which was launched soon after Suez, it was specifically explained that America intended to intervene if necessary in the Arab world to stop any communist penetration of the Middle East. The Arabs could not understand it. Many Arabs, quick as they were to see some conspiracy in the doctrine, saw it as a Zionist plot to discredit Arab nationalism by smearing it and automatically linking it with communism. Their suspicions about the Eisenhower doctrine were never allayed. The American and British landings in Lebanon and Jordan in 1958 did nothing to dispel the views of Arab nationalists that the West were still wishing to impose their policies upon the Arab world, and it was only a short step to assuming that their ulterior motive for wanting to wield such authority must be to relieve the Arab pressure on Israel. The various Western contradictions of Suez seemed to escape them, or else they were so caught in their own propaganda as to fail to see that the West were not working to anything resembling such a long-term plan, certainly not once the system of alliances collapsed with the overthrow of the Iraq regime in 1958.

With the overthrow of the Hashemite regime in Iraq in 1958 the force of anti-Westernism in the Middle East could be said to have succeeded in its main objectives. The American landings in Lebanon and British deployment to Jordan helped to prevent the collapse spreading to those countries. But after that date the main developments in Middle Eastern affairs were primarily internal ones, in the sense that the Western influence was only marginally relevant, and Soviet influence, though growing, was certainly not decisive at any time. Anti-Westernism remained a force, but the practical evidence to justify it became less easy to find.

The main developments concerned the formation and subsequent collapse of the union by Egypt and Syria into the United Arab Republic, and the later attempt to resume the union, this time with Iraq involved as well. The second phase ended in 1963, when the Arab world appeared to be riven by every possible political fissure. During this period Arab preoccupations with their own affairs resulted in little activity on the Israel front, other than the customary genuflections to the common goal of smashing Zionism. Zionism became just one more of the evil influences working on the Arab world, and certainly neither the most important nor the most pressing. Israel was occasionally used as an argumentative weapon to prove that one lot of Arabs were better pan-Arabs than the others, but there was no serious practical planning.

By the end of 1963 and early 1964 it was clear to most Arab governments, particularly, the Egyptian, Syrian and Iraq leaders, that any prospects for immediate unity were illusory, and that they would have to deal with each other, for better or for worse, as they were. This was particularly important from the Egyptian point of view, since it involved President Nasser accepting a certain degree of impotence to influence the Arab world the way he would have liked. He was also faced with a stalemate in his dispute with Saudi Arabia over the future of the Yemen. At such a cross-roads in Arab affairs, it was only natural that Israel returned to the top of the agenda, not so much because there was any substantial change in the position, but because Israel was always a convenient excuse in the Arab world. At that time, the near completion of Israel's diversion of the Jordan waters was the immediate excuse to galvanise the Arabs, but it could just as easily have been something else. It led to the formation of a Palestine Liberation Army among exiled Palestinians as an expression of the greater militancy of the Arabs as a whole, but that was as far as they were prepared to go.

From 1964 onwards the Soviet Union's influence can be discerned more and more in the Middle East, but not as a specifically anti-Israeli influence. The contradictions in the Soviet position and in the Arab positions normally meant that Israel was the only permanently safe currency for them to deal in. But their main objective, rather than the destruction of Israel, was to establish themselves as the dominant outside power in a region where the West had tried and failed to do the same.

It was probably more Soviet influence than anything which kept Egypt and Syria on speaking terms, in spite of the bitterness of the period following the collapse of the two attempts to form the United Arab Republic. The Soviet Union underwrote its initiatives with certain development projects, but more practically with large arms assistance programmes to the Arab armies, particularly in Syria and Egypt.

Whereas Egypt periodically attempted during this period to preserve some balance in her position by not totally discarding relations with the United States, Syria lurched, almost uncontrollably, further and further to the left. At first sight this may have appeared a godsend to Soviet policy, since each successive coup in Damascus seemed to make Syria that much more of a hostage to Moscow. But the unpredictable, volatile nature of

Syrian policies and politics made it just as unlikely that Russia would be able any more effectively to control Syria than Egypt had been able to do so with many more advantages during the period of the UAR.

Syria was permanently the pacemaker in the Arab world so far as hostility to Israel was concerned. Syrians were not content, like most of the rest of the Arab world, to accept that they were not powerful enough to give more weight to their hostility than that provided by the boycott of Israeli goods, the closure of the Suez Canal and the refusal to recognise Israel's existence. Syria followed this up with constant and repeated pinpricks on Israel, used not only to goad Israel into losing patience and doing herself political harm by excessive retaliation, but also to put the other Arab governments to shame by exposing their practical inactivity on the Israel issue.

There was no possibility, for instance, that Syria could achieve any military advantage against Israel. Nor were the Syrians unlikely to disagree with the rest of the Arabs that they were not capable at this stage of any effective military action against Israel. Continued irritation against Israel was, however, for Syria, a very useful way of making a point in the inter-Arab argument that was being conducted. It posed the rest of the Arab world with a horrible dilemma, since it undermined the whole of their general position that a successful outcome to Arab politics was the essential prerequisite to any concerted effort over Israel. Syria's actions against Israel specifically jeopardised that Arab solution, by casting doubt on the 'good Arabism' of any country which failed to come to her rescue if Israel retaliated. If the rest of the Arabs ignored Syria's anti-Israel actions, and the subsequent Israeli retaliation which was sure to follow, they were not only shelving the Arab-Israeli problem, they were also condemning to oblivion the movement towards more Arab co-operation. They appeared to be on an escalator which only Syria could stop.

But who could stop Syria ? Nobody, apparently. The Russians may have wanted to, but their relative inexperience in the Middle East, and their keenness to consolidate, had in effect made their position hopeless and their commitment over exposed. The

Egyptians, left to their own devices, would probably have ignored Syria, or at least outmanoeuvred her in the way President Nasser had repeatedly outmanoeuvred Damascus before. The Soviet presence in the area, however, made this prospect singularly unlikely. Syria had more or less played Iraq against Egypt, and vice-versa, in the inter-Arab politics of the area. It is fair to say that had she had only these two choices she would not, leading up to the 1967 crisis, have been in a position to provoke the whole Arab world into the military preparations which then took place. Her support from one or other of the capitals, Cairo or Baghdad, would have waned before that point had been reached. Soviet support for Syria, however, was automatically less easy to withdraw than any Arab support, just as Soviet control over Syria was probably less effective.

Inter-Arab arguments provided the background and the excuse for the rise in Arab-Israel temperature between 1965 and 1967. But it was the Soviet presence in the area, indirectly rather than directly and probably against Moscow's original intentions, which let Syria take the Arabs, against their better judgment, to the point where they collectively lost control of events.

6

The 1967 Build-up to War

THERE WERE seldom any new ingredients in the many crises
between the Arabs and Israel. Whenever there was a rise in
temperature, actions were based on one or other of the issues
which had divided the two sides since 1948—Jordan waters,
refugees, frontier security, or a combination of some or all of
them. Crises were normally precipitated when the natural balance provided by a variety of plots and a multiplicity of participants was upset.

The crisis of 1967 was not something absolutely sudden, since
the whole tempo, the whole rhythm, of the dispute had been
quickening since early 1966. This did not mean that any new
element was introduced, but simply that existing lines were more
sharply drawn, arguments were more bitterly pursued, tempers
and reputations became more frayed, so that the cycle of action,
reaction, recrimination and compromise became foreshortened
until there was no margin left for manoeuvre.

In the early part of the build-up, certainly between January
1966 and April 1967, the pace was more or less dictated by Syria
and Israel, with occasional interventions from Jordan. Since
Suez, of course, the ability of Egypt to control the pace of the
Israeli policy of the Arabs had been physically circumscribed by
the presence of the UN force between Egypt and Israel. President Nasser could and did make appropriate noises with his
army in Sinai, but never to the extent of promoting actual
operations across the frontier of the kind which continually took
place on the Israel, Syrian and Jordanian frontiers. This was
partly because the Egyptian army had since 1962 been pre-
occupied with the Yemen situation and South Arabia. But it also
reflected President Nasser's often expressed view that the Arab
world was not ready to take on Israel.

Syria and Jordan, however, with frontiers contiguous to Israel,
had through the years been able to provide actual proof of their

anti-Israeli stance in a way which President Nasser, in spite of his talk, was unable to do. Naturally, therefore, they were more likely to be the main elements in any early raising of the temperature, particularly as its purpose was primarily an inter-Arab argument rather than an anti-Israeli one.

In early 1966 the Syrian Government fell. The leftist wing of the leading Baath party ousted the rightist and more moderate wing, and Syrian politics then deteriorated. as did the frontier situation with Israel. Each skirmish, mining, or killing led, as usual, to retaliation. Eventually the United Nations in October said that both Syria and Israel had violated the armistice agreement in the demilitarised zone.

The Syrians were probably particularly sore at the fact that Israel had, through bombing, virtually destroyed the Syrian work on the water diversion project at Banias. Moreover, once that had been destroyed there was no installation of value on the frontier which would be vulnerable to Israeli retaliation. At the level of frontier warfare, therefore, they had little to lose from going on. The danger, as far as Syria was concerned, would be if Israeli retaliation was raised to overcome the fact that Syria was well fortified on the frontier and had little to lose. The Israeli response might, for instance, strike further into the country, and as though to guard against this they entered into a mutual defence pact with the Egyptians in November 1966.

Almost immediately after this the expected Israeli retaliation came. Only it came against Samu, a village in Jordan. Israeli troops in considerable strength crossed into Jordan early one morning and destroyed the town of Samu. Jordanians were evacuated by the soldiers, and their homes blown up. A Jordanian army column rushing to the rescue was ambushed and mauled, and then the Israelis withdrew. Why Jordan? There had been Jordanian raids earlier in the year, but Israel had already retaliated for those in April with the blowing up of houses, and some civilian casualties. Israel had also filed a complaint for a case of bombing in Jerusalem in September.

But the Samu raid had nothing to do with that. It was what nuclear strategists describe as an exemplary strike, in that the Israelis were making an example of Jordan to show Syria what

74

would happen if they went on, and to punish Jordan for allowing Syrian infiltrators to pass through Jordanian territory on their way to Israel. The raid, according to the UN announcement, caused 18 killed, 134 wounded and 127 buildings destroyed. It was in the classic tradition of Israeli retaliatory raids, with the only difference—and dangerous difference—that they were now prepared to extend it to punishing those who either actively or passively helped the terrorists, rather than simply punishing the country which provided the actual guerrilla base itself.

It was a new and not altogether justifiable doctrine, but obviously had the required effect on Jordan, whose King soon afterwards accused the Soviet Union of instigating unrest in the Middle East, presumably by her open and active support for Syria. The Israeli Foreign Minister also justified the raid about a month later by saying that the frequency of border incidents had diminished since it happened. Jordan, in response, gave permission for Iraqi and Saudi Arabian troops to cross Jordanian soil if the United Arab Republic asked the United Nations expeditionary force to leave Egypt, but King Hussein also refused to allow units of the Palestinian Liberation Army forces in Gaza to be stationed in Jordan.

This short period of comparative quiet ended early in January 1967 with clashes across the Jordan between Israel and Syria. Unexpectedly, both sides then agreed to an appeal by the UN Secretary-General to reconvene the mixed armistice commission which had not met in regular session since the dispute over the Huleh marshes in 1951. The meetings were not a success and early in February Israel sent another warning to Syria through diplomatic channels to the effect that a large retaliatory raid would be forthcoming if the border incursion from Syria did not stop. This warning was really superfluous since everybody in the Middle East knew that Israel retaliated for border raids and that retaliations increased in intensity and severity if the border raids continued.

Why then was this warning delivered? The Arabs are apt to see plots in everything, and immediately, on the strength of previous planned Israeli provocations, saw this as a prelude to a planned Israeli campaign against Syria. One cannot say at this stage whether that was so; most probably not, but if it was not so there is no particular justification for Israel's action, certainly in terms of adding a few degrees to the already heightened political temperature in the area.

The scale of operations against Syria expanded in early April when Israel sent in air-strikes to silence Syria's artillery which had been shelling Israeli tractors. The air-strikes were met by Syrian fighters, seven of which were knocked out in the ensuing battle. A few days later, the Prime Minister of Israel said in an interview that the United States Sixth Fleet in the Mediterranean would support Israel, and this was headlined in most Arab newspapers. It was assumed in most Arab capitals that there was a firm commitment on the part of the United States, which indeed there was, certainly to the extent of not seeing Israel 'driven into the sea' if that was at all conceivably possible. The realities of the military situation were, however, not likely to be very closely examined in the heady atmosphere which prevailed. Certainly as far as the great powers—Russia and America—were concerned the situation was by then polarised to the point where Russia was inalienably identified with the Arabs and the United States with Israel.

It is easy, of course, to censure Israel for being inflammable, or for making inflammable statements, when in fact nothing that Mr Eshkol said was nearly as inflammable as the Arabs were saying themselves. The trouble in the area was that whereas most statements were in fact made for internal domestic consumption they had also to be interpreted in neighbouring capitals. It is a common situation in international politics, and calls for qualities in national leaders which—if possessed—make them statesmen as opposed to mere politicians. That is more or less the difference between a statesman and a politician. The former is one who can, through leadership, guide and instruct his domestic following in the realities and limitations of his position outside the national boundaries. The latter is one who is pushed into certain external policies by the promptings of an electorate which cannot know the full story or appreciate the full details of the power relationships which exist outside.

Statesmanship was a quality which went by default in the

Middle East in the early months of 1967. President Nasser had shown it in the past when steering his people away from their much vaunted goal of smashing Israel. How else can one explain Egypt's openly avowed beliefs that the time was not ripe? Israel occasionally practised it, and indeed a policy of restraint had a certain historical tradition in Israel going back to the days of the Mandate when the Jewish community, led by the Jewish Agency, decided not to retaliate against Arab attacks but to leave the responsibility for so doing to the Mandate power. It was called the Havaglah (self-restraint) policy, and was only possible through tremendous self-discipline and will-power on the part of the Jews. The period after the Samu raid in late 1966 was one of the longest periods of self-restraint endured by official Israel, and may have been helped by a reduction in the number of forces which Egypt had stationed at El Arish in Sinai, behind the UN screen.

The last chapter of the crisis, before it erupted into war, probably started in early May of 1967. Mr Eshkol came out with the customary warnings that Israel would retaliate 'at a time and place of her own choosing' and with the appropriate means, against any interference in Jordan waters, sabotage, or the closure of the Gulf of Aqaba to Israeli shipping. There was nothing particularly new about these warnings, but the charged atmosphere of the moment appeared to give them greater significance. Or so the Syrians argued. The Syrian Government were anyway not in a healthy domestic position. It was not so much the time-honoured ruse of calling in an external threat to take people's minds off an internal crisis, or to unify support at home. That was intended for sure, only this time there was also some element of reality in the threat.

The Syrian regime was in an extremely vulnerable position, and it was conceivable that it would fall as a result of an Israeli action. It was anyway fairly weak on account of the obvious defeat sustained in the loss of seven MiG fighters in April. Syria's warnings were certainly based on something more than simply the need to goad Egypt into showing more physical support for Syria, or for making capital in the Arab world by pointing to Syrian militancy against Israel and the others' lack of it.

77

Through Soviet diplomats in Cairo, Egypt received reports that Israel was massing troops near to the Syrian frontier for a decisive blow against Syria. Later President Nasser referred to the fact that his aerial reconnaissance had located 18 Israeli brigades in the area. This assertion was probably based more on a deduction than on any real evidence. On what was this deduction based ? Probably, first, on the knowledge of previous Israeli tactics, which were to warn about retaliations and then wait for a suitable moment before striking. This sometimes involved setting up small situations, and the Israelis were prepared to wait some time for such favourable situations to develop. In the climate of the spring of 1967, however, no small action was going to be suitable. There was always an inevitable feeling of escalation about Israeli retaliations. There was no point, if one accepted their assumptions, in making the next blow less serious than the previous one, since the essence of the punitive approach was that it should serve as a deterrent for a while. If it was followed by more acts of terrorism, then obviously the punishment had not been strong enough.

These considerations were no secret. Therefore, on an examination of the scene from an Arab capital, and particularly from Damascus, the Arabs must have accepted that the more they goaded Israel the more likely it was that a heavy blow would be returned. That therefore provided the first, and reasonable, base for their suspicion that a heavy blow at Syria was being prepared—particularly as the last blow, at Jordan, had been shown not to have been successful in terms of stopping the Syrians.

Secondly, the deduction was based on more circumstantial evidence, according to the Syrians. In fact this evidence arose out of a ridiculous misunderstanding about the Israel independence parade which takes place annually in Jerusalem. The Israelis wanted to put on a big military show in Jerusalem, which they regard as their capital but which few other nations recognise as such. The Western powers applied great pressure on the Israel Government, as they do every year, to minimise the provocation which any Israeli military demonstration in Jerusalem is bound to cause in the Arab world, and which might anyway be held to violate the spirit if not the letter of the armistice agreement in which Jerusalem became a divided city, with a resident UN truce authority to supervise the division.

Israel eventually yielded to the Western pressure not to include tanks and armoured columns in the independence parade. But when these weapons did not appear the Arabs immediately assumed that it could only be because they were wanted and needed somewhere else, and where else could that be but on the Syrian frontier?

Against this background it was obviously important, in terms of Arab politics, for Egypt to do something. Indeed the more preparations he appeared to be taking to join Syria against Israel the more hope President Nasser had of exercising some control over Syria, and—more important—some control over a general situation which was getting out of hand.

President Nasser's immediate act was to put the army on an alert status, declare a state of emergency, and allow it to be reported that there were heavy troop movements going on. He went further, and asked for the United Nations forces to be withdrawn, presumably in response to the Arab taunts, including some from Jordan, that he was using the UNEF force as his alibi, and that he was sheltering behind the UN so that he could be protected from Israel.

Surprisingly for most of the world, the UN Secretary-General agreed to the removal of the forces and ordered their withdrawal. There has been much discussion about the wisdom and legality of his act. As far as the legality of it is concerned, although it appears that any alteration of the status of the UN force should have been accompanied by consultation with other interested powers at the UN, there seems to be no doubt that Egypt, in the final analysis, must have possessed a sovereign right in an emergency to ask the UN force to withdraw from Egyptian territory, such as Sharm el Sheikh. So far as the Gaza strip was concerned however—not officially Egyptian territory, but simply territory mandated to Egypt under the terms of the 1949 armistice—there is probably more doubt. There certainly seems to have been enough doubt to have justified U Thant delaying his immediate acceptance of the Egyptian demands,

and the promptness with which he accepted them probably surprised Cairo as much as it surprised everybody else.

On this occasion President Nasser displayed surprisingly little
wisdom. The balance of legality was probably on his side, but
the wisdom of pursuing a course of policy, even accepting that
he was within his rights, was questionable, particularly when
put against his well-grounded knowledge of Israeli power and
the likely Israeli reaction to such a situation. In his acts during
that critical fortnight he showed more misjudgment than
illegality. It would not be right, therefore, to portray him as a
man who pursued a criminal, illegal and warmongering course.
He was right—legalistically—but even in human situations, let
alone in international affairs, there are times when to be right is
not necessarily to be either prudent or safe.

Developments in the last phase of the crisis can be broadly put
under three headings—the internal politics of the Arab world;
the internal politics within Israel; and the international attempts
to intervene and influence the course of the crisis from outside.
These were all proceeding more or less independently of each
other, but they all had some effect on the development of those
two weeks.

First of all, in the Arab world, President Nasser's coup
against the UN helped him to regain the initiative in Arab
politics which he had definitely not possessed—not to that extent
—for about three years. Moreover it did so in the context of an
anti-Israel act which made it politically impossible for anybody
else in the Arab world to question either his actions or leadership. The collapse of those Arab regimes with moderate views
on Israel in the 1940s and 1950s was enough of a lesson for
modern Arab governments to heed, however irrelevant they may
have thought the Israeli issue was.

The Arab bandwagon started rolling, and this made it necessary for other Arabs to commit themselves, not only verbally
but also by carrying out appropriate military movements to show
their practical willingness to go along with the crowd. Iraq,
Jordan and Kuwait placed their troops on the alert. Twelve Arab
nations, excluding Tunisia, released a joint declaration that an

attack against any one of them would be considered an attack against them all. Jordan's king flew to Cairo to sign a defence pact with Egypt. All these gestures had in fact been carried out several times before in times of Arab fervour over Israel—the joint declarations, the assignment of all armies to one command, and so on—but practice in their manoeuvres had nevertheless failed in the past to prove their actual worth in terms of co-ordination of strategy or military unification. There was once again the appearance of Arab unity, however, which was a great psychological asset from the point of view of propaganda in an area where psychology and propaganda have long taken the place of practical diplomacy.

Arab politics had acquired a head of steam. It would have called for statesmanlike qualities to succeed in arranging for the momentum to die down slightly without singular loss of face. Again the essence of statesmanship should be to avoid getting into a situation from which there is absolutely no political alternative to proceeding on a set course if that course becomes evidently more dangerous. It is perhaps a measure of President Nasser's lost prestige in the Arab world between 1963 and 1967 that he was obviously less able to deflect or defuse a situation than he had been. The momentum of the crisis in internal Arab terms drove him on, from evicting the UN force to announcing the closure of the Gulf of Aqaba to Israeli shipping, although he knew that ten years earlier, in 1957, the Israeli Government had said that they would regard such an act as an act of aggression, which would merit an appropriate response.

What then was the effect in Israel of the Arab manoeuvring? The Israelis have always been prone to take Arab posturings at their face value in spite of many years' experience now of the invalidity of most Arab positions. We know of their retaliatory policy, and we know that, as explained by General Rabin in 1965 (and indeed by General Dayan in 1955) the *psychology* of Middle East politics was as much regarded as a military consideration as the actual deployment of troops or any equation about the relative ability of any or all of the Arabs to wage effective war against Israel. We know therefore that either a real or psychological alteration in the situation was regarded as a threat to

Israel's security which must not go unheeded—and it did not seem to matter whether the alteration was only psychological.

We know too that the tradition of Israeli strategy was in fact to pre-empt any such change, or certainly redress it before it became consolidated. Any change in the status quo at that time was therefore regarded by Israel as dangerous and unacceptable, and it was a reasonable assumption that, unless dissuaded or prevented, she would do all she could by force to prevent such a change happening. The justification for this attitude will be examined in a little more detail in the next chapter, but from the narrative point of view it had the following effect on Israeli politics internally and on Israeli actions externally.

Internally, most Israelis were conditioned into believing that Israel's best policy was to act and act quickly against the Arabs. That was the meaning of their quick mobilisation schemes, practised over the years. That was the meaning of the big defence budget which they had to pay. That was the general political acceptance of the siege attitude to Israel's security, and to her political position in the Middle East, because, as we have seen, there was little distinction made between the two.

On the other hand, there were constraints on Israel action. One was the need for a little time, certainly a week or ten days, to reach the highest point of military effectiveness. The other was the limited but nevertheless accountable factor of international opinion, which Israel wanted on her side. In the end they became complementary, because the need for a week or ten days' military preparations satisfactorily coincided with the time which was also needed to pay some attention to international opinion.

We know of Israel's previous reluctance to have international supervision of her dealings with the Arab world because of the limitations it would obviously impose on her own freedom of action. It was this which accounted for her refusal to invite the UNEF into her side of the territory after it had been expelled from Egypt. We know also that Israel had, of course, an American guarantee that she would be protected in the event of an invasion, and there was no doubting that guarantee, whether or not other attempts at international action were successful. On the other hand, against all her traditions and all her expectations, Israel participated at least momentarily in the international political attempts to influence the crisis. With the benefit of hindsight, it seems that her participation was more governed by a desire to gain time until she was ready to go it alone than by any genuine belief in the worth of diplomacy at that stage.

Basically, international action during the crisis was centred on the American attempts to drum up international support for reaffirmation of the right of free passage through the Gulf of Aqaba. Most nations with maritime interests had signed the Geneva Convention of 1958 which affirmed this right. But the Arab world had not done so, and the inclusion of the specific clause which applied to the Gulf of Aqaba was, in fact, unconstitutional since it had been added later and had not been in the generally accepted draft prepared by international lawyers. There was therefore no particularly strong legal case for co-operating with the Americans. Moreover, what were the prospects of enforcing such a declaration, assuming that Egypt continued to maintain her rights, which were certainly in the legal sense entitled to a hearing? Most maritime nations flinched from doing this, but Great Britain co-operated closely with the United States and actually reached a stage when naval planning for such an operation was begun.

The other international influences were primarily from France, and then Russia. France, contrary to most people's expectations, declared a policy of complete neutrality in the affair. This may have seemed difficult, since most of Israel's air force consisted of French aircraft and there had been close military co-operation between France and Israel since even before the 1956 Suez collusion, but in the context of France's attempt to make her peace with the Arab world it was a consistent stance. Where President de Gaulle misjudged the situation was in thinking that by siding with the Arabs (while Britain and America obviously sided more with Israel) this act alone would preserve a Great Power balance and provide for some Great Power co-operation in solving the dispute. He did not believe that without France's hostility to America there would be any chance of the United

States and the Soviet Union coming together over the Middle East, because of the disruptive effects on their relationship caused by Vietnam. In this he was wrong. As it subsequently turned out—admittedly after the war but very soon after it—there had been constant and clear assurances flowing between Washington and Moscow to the effect that both sides had an interest not only in preserving peace but, in the event of a breakdown of peace, in not getting involved in a war.

The outbreak of fighting showed up the singular inability of any outside power to control events in the Middle East during a crisis. Great Powers could be an influence at other times, and in the case of the Soviet Union an increasing influence, whereas in the case of the West a declining one. But they were not in a position to control events, and it was perhaps this realisation more than anything which governed their separate determination to stay as much as possible outside an area in which they might get sucked into circumstances which were obviously beyond their control.

International opinion seems to have been at fault in believing that there was anything that outside influence could do at the time. It was certainly the view in Israel that nothing was going to stop them. Probably the only thing which would have stopped them would have been a specific, positive declaration by the United States and Britain that they would go to the help of the Arabs—that they were indeed already on the Arabs' side—and that was not only politically impossible in both those countries but the opposite had already been shown to be their attitudes in public statements made earlier that May.

The UN Security Council debate which was called in the last days before war was inconclusive. The armada of maritime nations was quite obviously never going to materialise. The breathing space called for by the United States appeared likely to pass very soon. On Monday, June 5, fighting broke out between Egypt and Israel, started by a devastating Israeli air attack which virtually destroyed the Egyptian air force and paved the way for military advances against Egypt exactly similar to, only even more convincing than, the Sinai campaign of 1956. At the end of four days Israel was in charge of the entire Sinai peninsula.

Elsewhere, the Syrian and Jordanian air forces had also been knocked out when they joined in the fighting. Israel had captured the entire West Bank of the Jordan, which was Jordanian-held Palestine, and the heights on the Syrian frontier from which Syrian artillery had constantly bombarded Israeli farm settlements in Galilee. It was the end of another round.

7

Why War?

AS A RESULT of fighting against the Arabs in June 1967 Israel won another battle, but it could not be said that she had won the war. The battle of 1967 brought no immediate sign of any solution with it. Peace—a real politically adjusted peace as opposed to a military ceasefire—seemed as far away as ever.

Wars bring unnatural adjustments to international affairs. They are more often started by accident or miscalculation than by design. On the other hand the belligerents normally have some idea why they start fighting—either what they want to gain from doing so or what they want to prevent the other side gaining—while they would probably accept that within those limits the eventual outcome could be very different from what was originally expected by either side.

One must ask oneself, therefore, what the Israelis expected to gain from the war, or what they thought they were preventing the Arabs gaining. Did Israel believe that there was any final, lasting objective to be gained, and if so what was it? By and large the people of Israel want their nation to be recognised by the Arabs and then to be left in peace. The majority of them would therefore feel that any breakdown in peace was not of their doing, but was the almost exclusive responsibility of the Arabs. They would argue that a permanent peace could be quite simply achieved if the Arabs would only agree with them. They would be unwilling to accept that their own internal policies could or should affect the attitudes of those around them, and would reject the view that there is any sort of innate Israeli belligerence which itself stimulates the Arabs to belligerence. They would be either unaware, or unwilling to acknowledge, any historical obligation to adapt themselves more to the sensitivities of their neighbours. Indeed for too many of them history still holds memories of previous attempts to assimilate with their surroundings, in Western societies, the failure of which most probably resulted in their emigration to Israel in the first place.

So, apart from a few radically inclined circles in Israel, the general Israeli approach to the future went little further than the prevailing status quo, but without the Arabs' hostility. If that hostility could not be voluntarily withdrawn by the Arabs, then the limit of Israeli ambition was for security through strength. They would suffer Arab provocations until they became intolerable. When Israeli patience was exhausted, they would hit back hard and force the Arabs to drop their active hostility—at least for a while.

This punitive approach to the Arabs was normally adopted more in sorrow than in anger, coupled with the wish and apparent belief among some Israelis that the Arabs themselves would sooner or later realise the futility of their policy and drop their hostility to Israel. But, failing recognition by the Arabs, failing any acceptance by them of a Zionist Israel, failing any Israeli acceptance of a non-Zionist Israel—even, say, of the principle of a bi-national state in Palestine—this kind of comparative peace was the most that Israel could hope for.

In the weeks before fighting began in June 1967 I spoke to many Israeli citizens in Tel Aviv, Jerusalem and up and down the country. There was an almost uncanny unanimity about them. They were fatalistic about war. They believed that it had to come. It would possibly only bring them a decade of reasonable peace before they had to fight again, yet even that period was worth fighting for. They were in a 'no alternative' situation. If they did not fight then, they would only have to fight on worse terms later on. They argued and believed, that their national survival was at stake. In a society normally so critical, so disparate in its opinions, so persistently introspective and questioning, the categorical nature of this attitude was extraordinary. Among the many voices of Israel, there was no voice which questioned this conventional wisdom. As far as the great mass of her citizens was concerned, war was inevitable. In such a situation it seemed only natural to forgo argument and leave the rest to the generals.

It is difficult at the best of times for an outsider to question a nation's own view of its national interest and its own opinions of what does and does not constitute a threat to its national survival. From the point of view of the outside world, I believe that it was already too late to argue with Israel about the nature of the threat against her. Israeli society was convinced of the threat, and this total conviction was the product of years of unconscious conditioning. In 1967 there was no persuasion that any outside power could exert on Israel to induce her to reassess the position, or to accept somebody else's judgment about the situation.

The decision to fight which was taken early that June had in essence been taken long before. It was taken in many ways and at many times between 1948 and 1967. It was a continuation of the decision taken in 1956 to launch the Sinai campaign. It was the same decision which was taken each time Israel ordered a retaliatory act, only on a much larger scale. It is a decision which will probably be taken again, and indeed has already been taken since the war, for instance in the Israeli reaction to the sinking of their destroyer by the Egyptians—an act which provoked them to destroy the Egyptians' oil refinery at Suez—and in the attack on Jordan at the end of March, 1968. It is a popular decision with the majority of the people of Israel, and any change in the policy can only flow from a change in the Israeli attitude itself and not from the promptings of any outside power so long as Israel remains the dominant military power in the area.

I do not believe, however, that the specific assumption that there was no alternative for Israel but to go to war stands up to a close examination, and I shall hope to show why not. To reach this conclusion, one must analyse the real threats, and the worst possible consequences of not immediately reacting to them in the way that Israel did.

I see the threats as threefold. There was the military threat which sprang from the frequently declared intention of the Arabs to invade Israel and slaughter the Jews, and which had to be assessed in terms of the ability of the Arab armed forces either to carry out this threat or to achieve something so little short of it as to amount to the virtual destruction of Israel as a modern state. There was the economic threat, which was based on the Arabs' frequently declared intention to destroy Israel economically, or, by crippling her economy, to reduce her ability to defend herself and so undermine Israeli society that the country would be irretrievably weakened. Finally, there was the psychological threat that, unless checked by Israel, the Arabs would come to believe their own extravagant propaganda, and would assume that they could get away with an ever-increasing amount of provocation against Israel. These were the threats; had they so intensified in 1967 that war was unavoidable?

Of course there *was* a threat to Israel at that time. The political and military temperature in the area had risen appreciably. There was an increased risk of fighting either through miscalculation or through misunderstanding. But an increased risk, such as there was, does not necessarily entitle one of the parties concerned to assume that there is nothing left for it but to take immediate preventive action against the possibility of the risk increasing further. Israelis might argue that their government in that situation had a duty to take the action which was most likely to decrease the danger to the people of Israel, or at least to see that they did not emerge from the period of danger in a worse position than they had entered it. One could also argue however that in making a decision to go to war—particularly pre-emptive war—in a situation of great risk, one is automatically committing a nation to a course of action the end of which nobody can foresee; unless, that is, the decision is based on the most precise military appreciation and confidence of the outcome.

There was, after all, an increased risk of war during the Cuba confrontation between Russia and the United States; there was an increased risk in the Berlin crisis; there is always a risk, and sometimes a greatly increased risk, of war between India and Pakistan over Kashmir, or Greece and Turkey over Cyprus, and many other situations where the diplomatic process seems to have come near to the point of exhaustion, leaving no alternative open but recourse to arms.

On which criterion was the Israeli decision based in 1967? Given that they thought the situation was critical to the overall security of Israel, had they reached the stage at which they thought that the risk was so great that it exceeded their natural impulse to avoid precipitating something whose outcome they could only guess at ? Or were their military calculations so precise that they knew more or less how they would emerge from such a conflict ? Which of these formed the basis for their decision to discard all further political attempts to defuse the crisis ? If it was the second, they must therefore have known there was no real threat in the first place, otherwise their calculations could hardly have been that confident. But if one acquits them of that kind of premeditated attack, then one must convict them of launching their country into a dangerous escapade, with only a vague idea of its possible outcome.

On balance, I believe one must assume that the Israel Government went to war on the basis of a reasonably confident calculation that they would come out of it in an improved position from that which obtained in May 1967. One cannot believe that if they had not been certain of their military superiority they would have taken a decision which, without that superiority, would have endangered Israel far more than a decision *not* to fight would have done at that stage.

No responsible government would go to war unless reasonably confident of victory or unless faced with the alternative prospect of total defeat without a shot being fired. Israel claimed, of course, that it was that very prospect which faced her in May 1967. But the Israelis have consistently thought themselves into a position where their national survival appears to be under a much greater threat than it really is. This has caused them, as a nation, to see each crisis as presenting much too stark a set of alternatives, between total defeat and total victory, when the situation has been much less extreme. If they were reasonably confident of some kind of limited success from attacking the Arabs, how much more confident should they have been of their ability, in defence, to prevent the Arabs carrying out a real attack on them ?

The military equation between Israel and her neighbours has been portrayed as a small nation of two-and-a-half million people surrounded by a hostile ring of about forty million Arabs bent on her destruction—odds of twenty to one against Israel.

On paper this might look impressive, but no military assessment of the comparative power of countries can be based simply on population figures, or even, for that matter, on the listed number of men in the armed forces. The whole war machine is much harder to assess, but it must obviously include the industrial capability of the country as much as the equipment of the armed forces, their ability to use that equipment, and the administrative and logistical competence of the regular staff in keeping the armed forces properly organised and supplied for battle.

Another factor which cannot be ignored is the nature of the terrain over which any campaign is likely to be fought. Perhaps most important of all is the maintenance of a clear and unequivocal political objective for the troops themselves. In spite of the increasing technicality of warfare, a well-educated and well-indoctrinated army is still a match for better equipped and more numerous opponents if they lack the necessary motivation.

On paper, in spite of the minority of population, Israel's war machine is by no means at a twenty-to-one disadvantage when compared to the Arabs. By dint of a superbly orchestrated system of reserves, Israel could in the space of a few days put a modern well-trained army of 250,000 men into the field. At the start of the war this was certainly not less than the total number of troops available to the Arab countries on her borders. According to American intelligence, which a few days before the war made a very accurate prediction of the likely outcome of any fighting, there were six Egyptian divisions in the Sinai Desert totalling 81,000 men, faced by at least 100,000 Israelis. The Jordanian and Syrian armies could only produce as a grand total about 40,000 and 50,000 respectively. An Iraqi division of about 12,000 men was thought to be on its way to Jordan. There was thus no question of the Israeli armed forces being outnumbered by the Arab armies facing them, even on the most pessimistic assessment of the mobilisation of the Arab armies. Those figures after all assumed that both the Jordanian and Syrian regimes were in a position to commit their entire land forces to a campaign outside their own frontiers. Apart from the geographical and administrative difficulties which this would entail, it is a possibility which also ignores the unlikelihood, politically speaking, of either of those regimes being confident enough of internal security within their countries to allow their armies to be so totally occupied elsewhere.

Apart from the absence of any numerical inferiority, Israel had other geographical and tactical advantages. She had the internal lines of communication, the ability to switch forces quickly from one front to the other, the central command which would not, as in the Arab case, be bedevilled in an emergency by conflicting orders and the possible clash of political directives from the various governments involved. The geographical difficulties in mounting a serious and sustained land offensive into Israel would be formidable. Egypt's lines of communication would have to stretch back across the Sinai Desert. Nor would it have been easy to transfer a large part of the Egyptian army to Jordan to launch an attack into the narrow waist of Israel. The Jordanian army would be swamped logistically by having to provide the necessary services for a foreign army as large as, if not larger than, itself.

Even accepting that some way would be found, is it conceivable that King Hussein would play host to a force of that size which could so easily, and so irrevocably, turn into an army of occupation? Nor, geographically, was a Syrian invasion into Israel likely to prosper for very long. Any thrust would have to come over the various crossings of the Jordan which were well covered by the Israelis. The Syrian dispositions seemed to show, anyhow, that Syria herself, having realised the difficulties which would attend any real advance into Israel, was satisfied instead with artillery bombardments from what she thought were impregnable defensive positions in the heights above the frontier.

I have so far excluded air power from this argument because I believe that the problems which would attend any land invasion of Israel by the Arab forces would attend that invasion whether or not they had air superiority. Before going on to consider the other possible threat to Israel's security—loss of her air power—it was necessary to show the basic impracticability of a land campaign against Israel regardless of the air situation.

The air forces of the two sides—Israel on the one hand, the

Arabs on the other—were more or less evenly balanced, with both possessing about 400-450 strike aircraft of varying size and performance. The Arabs probably had a marginal numerical majority—perhaps about fifty planes—and certainly Egypt's best aircraft were better than Israel's best. But against this could be held the much higher standard of training of the Israeli pilots and almost undoubtedly higher serviceability of their aircraft.

One cannot say that either side had a decisive superiority in the air. If one could imagine a war between the two sides without either air force being seriously depleted through being caught in advance on the ground, there would probably have been a reasonable balance of power in the air. If both air forces had been able to survive a surprise attack by the other side and knew that they could, this mutual deterrence might have resulted in a situation where a land battle would have been fought without the benefit of any decisive air superiority one way or the other.

But from the Israeli point of view, the conditions of May and June 1967 made air supremacy an absolute prerequisite of any campaign. The existence of large formations of troops on Israel's frontiers meant that it was likely to be more difficult to make any decisive advance against them in the limited number of days which would be available before world opinion forced an end to the fighting. The opportunities for decisive action were only possible if Israel had a complete, or almost complete, mastery of the air. A land campaign conducted under conditions in which evenly balanced air forces merely contributed to the tactical engagements would be a slow process and quite unsuitable to Israel's requirements. Israel had to achieve a decisive victory in the shortest time possible to give her some political and territorial advantages for the period after the war.

As we saw, the Egyptian air force in reality was unable to survive a surprise attack on it by the Israelis, who did not wait themselves to find out whether they would have been similarly vulnerable from an Egyptian strike. In fact, the Israeli air force practises the same vigilance that permeates the rest of Israel's approach to the military situation, and there has been a permanent air-borne alert of Israeli aircraft in operation for some years.

It does not consist of many aircraft, but at least makes certain that the whole of Israel's air force could not be destroyed by the kind of brilliantly planned and executed surprise attack which the Israelis themselves carried out on the Egyptians. Israel's three military airfields are, however, only a few seconds' flying time from her borders. And in assessing the threat one must consider the worst possible situation which could befall Israel, which would be the destruction of her air force by just such an Arab attack.

What would happen then? It would not be correct to assume that an Arab advance into Israel could be quite so swift, even with Arab air superiority, as was the Israeli advance across the desert into Egypt, for various reasons including those which I have already mentioned. The land in Israel is not so pitilessly exposed as the desert. It is possible, though obviously more difficult, to fight without air cover. The Egyptians fled from the desert when they lost their air forces, because they had somewhere else to go. For an Israeli army there would be no alternative but to stand and fight. To that must be added the fact that any invasion force which penetrated into Israel would not simply have Israel's 250,000 strong army to contend with, although it alone would probably be stronger than the invaders. The entire nation, with a labour force of more than 900,000, could be expected to take up arms and fight.

Many Israelis would argue that they could not afford even to consider that kind of possibility because the Arabs had openly avowed their intention to rape and kill if they ever succeeded in invading Israel. The thought of this undoubtedly spurred the Israeli armed forces on during the fighting, and yet it also throws up the paradox in the whole military question. There was, and always has been, this curious contradiction between the Israelis' readiness to take on apparently insuperable odds outside their country in order to prevent something happening inside their country, which by definition would be an easier task to tackle than the former.

Finally, there was the threat of Arab bombing of civilian targets and population centres in Israel. Of course it was absolutely possible to bomb any target in Israel from any of her Arab neigh-

94

bours, which were only a few minutes' flying time from Tel Aviv and the narrow and densely populated waist of Israel. Israel has a small anti-aircraft missile system, but one which could quite easily be saturated by the number of aircraft against her. The Egyptians also claimed to have missiles which they could fire at Israel, although there has been no evidence that they were operational, and their accuracy, even if operational, was such that they were just as likely to land in Jordan as in Israel. The final threat of bombardment of Israeli cities came from the existence of Egypt's navy, which was equipped with missile-firing launches made in the Soviet Union. The prospect of Tel Aviv being hit by one or all of these weapons was certainly taken very seriously by Government and citizen alike, and civil defence precautions such as the sandbagging of doorways, building of air-raid shelters, and a total blackout, were all carried out right the way through the war.

The main point about this threat, however, is that Israel had no specific defence against it. In common with many other countries who share a frontier with a potentially hostile neighbour, the speed of jet aircraft and of missiles made it inconceivable that such a blow could be prevented in advance. Israel's defence was her ability to retaliate—and it was this alone which would deter the Arabs from launching such an attack. That is why I do not believe there is any point in trying to divorce this question of bombing Tel Aviv from the overall military equation, because such an act could not be carried out in isolation, and would obviously have been regarded as an act of war worthy of the fullest retribution of the kind which Israel meted out anyway. What I am suggesting, however, is that the mere threat of this happening is not something which on its own should justify a surprise attack on Egypt's airfields. It creates a dangerous precedent in the Middle East, and not only in the Middle East but in any other area of tension, that the mere existence of a potentially hostile bomber force, within range, in itself justifies a country carrying out a pre-emptive strike without waiting for any more positive proof of belligerence.

The fact of the matter is that the Arabs were not very likely to bomb Israel unless they were confident they could get away with it in all respects, and this they quite clearly could not guarantee. The threat of Arab bomb attacks on Israel cities was no more or less real than the threat of Israel doing the same to the Arabs as a reprisal.

I have attempted to make the point that the idea that Israel was at any time in danger of being 'driven into the sea' is a myth. Bearing in mind the Arabs' capacity for make-believe—at least in their propaganda—it is important to resist the temptation to take their openly voiced intentions at face value. It is true that Israel has much documentary evidence to illustrate the odious way in which the Arabs attempt to indoctrinate their school-children with the wish to annihilate Israel, and this has obviously increased the climate of bitterness and aggression between the two peoples. But even given a token wish on the part of the Arabs to erase the Jews from Palestine; even given the unlikely, if not absolutely inconceivable, event of their being able to co-ordinate their political objectives and arrive at a common strategy towards Israel; even given that Arab Governments would, uncharacteristically, decide they were able to spare enough soldiers for that kind of operation outside their own territories; they would still be a long way from the defeat and physical eradication of Israel as a modern state.

States are not so easily liquidated. The Germans were able to commit genocide, but only within their own country. And those Jews who went to the slaughter chambers had no frontier tradition to fall back on such as exists in modern Israel; they were not steeped in the guerrilla warfare and terrorism which had paved Israel's ascent to nationhood; they had no universal conscription and para-military upbringing on agricultural settlements such as young men and women in Israel have today.

But if, in spite of their propaganda, the Arab intention in 1967 was not to drive Israel into the sea, what was it?

As late as the spring of 1967, President Nasser was still saying that the Arabs were not ready to take on Israel, and that statement presumably reflected the advice of his military leaders as much as his own judgement. We can assume that his military capability had not marginally changed in the ensuing few months

96

before the crisis of May and June. But it is now fairly obvious that the speed of political developments during those weeks outpaced the ability of the military command in Cairo to keep up with them.

An Egyptian army was permanently stationed in Sinai, and to this President Nasser merely added reinforcements in May and moved their positions further east to replace the United Nations forces. But the speed with which they were moved into Sinai made it unlikely that they would be prepared for an offensive campaign, and indeed their subsequent deployment and activity seemed to confirm that they were supposed to take up deep defensive positions. But although their defences were far from complete, and their tactics were largely untried, President Nasser either ignored, or was ignorant of the fact, that his armed forces were not at that stage capable of providing the military backing which was necessary for the policy he was following.

That policy was plainly set out on May 26 in the Cairo newspaper *Al Ahram*, which normally reflects the views of the Government. The editor wrote, 'I am confident that for many reasons, chiefly the psychological, Israel cannot accept or remain indifferent to what has taken place. It has to deal a blow. We have to be ready for it, to minimise its effects as much as possible. Then it will be our turn to deal the second blow, which we will deliver with the utmost possible effectiveness.'

There could hardly have been a clearer explanation of the Arab strategy. They were trying to box in Israel, to goad her into making the first move by striking out, when they would be ready to cushion the blow, and then hit back hard themselves. As it turned out, the flaw in this policy was that the Arab armed forces, or more particularly the Egyptian armed forces, were in no position to ride the Israeli blow and failed dismally to 'minimise its effects'. These were, in fact, so devastating that the Arabs never got their second chance.

In theory, however, the policy was sound. The pattern of Israeli reaction to Arab hostility was by then predictable. In response to Arab provocations, the Israelis were accustomed to retaliate harder. The Arab intention, presumably, was therefore to build up a ring of forces round Israel so that she would have that much more difficulty in dealing any effective blow in retaliation. The goading on the frontiers would then go on, and Israel would either be forced to sustain a psychological defeat by not retaliating, or else be forced to strike out in the manner predicted by *Al Ahram*, with the risk that the Egyptian forces would be ready to ride the blow and come back with a devastating second strike of their own. Presumably Israel intelligence, which has thoroughly penetrated the Arab governments, had ascertained that the Egyptian forces were indeed not prepared for the policy which had been set out by the Egyptian leadership. This knowledge probably swayed the Israeli leadership in favour of a decision to strike, rather than risk the psychological defeat of allowing the situation to develop further unchallenged.

I have endeavoured to show that the actual military threat to Israel was not imminent, either in terms of an invasion of Israel, or of an air attack on her cities. The military threat, if it had existed at all, would have lain in the way Israel reacted to the Arab manoeuvring, since she was in theory falling into a trap by so reacting. She was able to spring the trap, however, because the Egyptians were not ready to set it. Of course they would not have been able to set it in the first place but for the rigidity of Israel's military policy over the years, which placed such a premium on the necessity to keep the psychological initiative by instant major retaliation against every Arab provocation.

Even without the military argument, however, there were other psychological and economic reasons for going to war. The economic threat was twofold. It came from the closure of the Gulf of Aqaba and the disruptive economic effects of a prolonged military crisis during which Israel had to keep a large part of her civilian labour force under arms. The economic importance of Eilat had increased enormously since 1956, when Israel opened up the Gulf. The port had expanded and with it the volume of Israel's exports to markets in Africa, Asia and Australia. In the wake of this trade, Israel was also making valuable political penetrations which she hoped would result in a much wider group of countries favourably inclined to her case at the United Nations.

When set against Israel's overall economic performance,

however, Eilat was still only of marginal importance. Five per cent of her exports went through Eilat, and closure of the Gulf, though discomforting, was not something which was going to cripple Israel overnight. In fact it could be presented economically as no more, and probably less, damaging to Israel than the damage done to Britain caused by the subsequent closure of the Suez Canal.

Eilat was also important because most of Israel's oil imports from Iran were unloaded there and pumped through a pipeline to the Mediterranean coast. Before Eilat was built, Israel had to supplement her own small oil production by importing oil from the United States and South America. Since the opening of the Gulf of Aqaba, and the use of Eilat, she had managed to build up stockpiles for at least nine months' self-sufficiency, even after supplies were cut off. During that time alternative sources could obviously be brought into play.

The other economic threat to Isreal was potentially more serious, but less direct. It was caused by Israel's mobilisation scheme, which involved bleeding the civilian labour force to keep reservists on active duty in the armed forces. Even if the Egyptian army in Sinai was not offensively deployed, Israel obviously could not ignore it, and as long as it remained there in such strength Israel would have to keep an equivalent force on her side of the frontier. This would mean the constant activation of some of her reservists. Mobilisation was an expensive business for Israel. She was able to field such a large army only by drawing heavily on the civilian labour force. Her whole mobilisation scheme, like the rest of her strategy, was geared to a plan which called for the maximum military and economic effort over the shortest possible time. Provided she saw to it that each crisis was a short one, she could afford this high degree of mobilisation. The economy was so organised that it could stand the effect of a momentary sharp disruption, but not the erosion of a long campaign.

One should remember, however, that, in spite of this, only about one quarter of Israel's labour force was actually called up into the armed forces, and even within that mobilisation plan every effort was made to spare the essential services and the country's key industries. It would not be correct therefore, to say that it was economically *impossible* for Israel to survive any crisis other than one of short duration. A longer crisis would obviously impose more strain on an economy which in 1967 was already in need of careful supervision, but the point to be emphasised is that Israel had specifically chosen to organise her manpower that way and could therefore just as easily adjust it to some other basis. She had specifically chosen to gear her mobilisation scheme for the maximum short-term advantage, in the full knowledge that this choice must limit her freedom of manoeuvre in any military crisis.

One of the effects of the 1967 crisis has been to induce the Israeli leadership to devise an alternative mobilisation scheme which is less inhibiting, particularly where time is concerned. They are now examining how to use their manpower more flexibly so that they can maintain a reasonably high standard of military preparedness over a much longer period of tension without feeling overwhelming economic pressure to put an end to the crisis as quickly as possible.

But although there obviously was great industrial pressure on the Israeli Government to finish off the crisis before it seriously endangered the economy, one cannot say that the economic danger on its own was really so critical that it justified going to war. Like the other pressures on Israel, as an individual threat it did not amount to a valid cause of war. The question is, did the combination of threats—although individually invalid—as a whole justify the decision to strike out?

I believe that the deciding factor was undoubtedly a psychological one, and in that, at least, the editor of *Al Ahram* was not wrong in his predictions. What were the psychological reasons which prevented Israel from allowing a longer period for political attempts to defuse the crisis to be tried? Obviously, if Israel were confident of reaping certain advantages from a battle there would be little interest in taking the heat out of the crisis. But I would like to give the Israeli Government the benefit of the doubt, at least to the extent of assuming that they must have considered the possibility of sitting out the crisis for longer, before eventually deciding in favour of war.

What, after all, had happened that was of such psychological significance? President Nasser had by a few diplomatic manoeuvres reversed the defeat of Sinai and reverted to a position similar to that which Egypt had occupied in 1955. Shipping to and from Eilat was stopped and the whole diplomatic initiative appeared to be back in President Nasser's hands for the first time in years—ten years as far as the Israeli question was concerned and about four years within the Arab world itself.

The Egyptian decision to close the Gulf to Israeli shipping was not a popular one with the rest of the maritime world, and in view of Israel's known attitude it was provocative to the point of folly. But it was certainly arguable in international law, and if there was supportable legal justification for such an act should not Israel's declaration that it was a *casus belli* have been regarded as just as questionable, just as precipitate, as the Egyptian act itself? Psychologically, Israel was reluctant to let the challenge go by without an immediate answer, just as she was reluctant to face the prospect of having to admit that the arms build-up on her frontiers would make it hard for her to retaliate against the Arab provocations in her own time and at a place of her choosing.

As it was, Israel was remarkably quick to exhaust the diplomatic process before deciding to discard it in favour of going to war. Indeed the only diplomacy attempted was the Anglo-American suggestion that the maritime nations should somehow enforce the principle of free passage through the Gulf of Aqaba —a doubtful venture which never left the ground. The possibility of sweating out the crisis while other formulae were examined was rejected out of hand by Israel on the psychological grounds that failure to react then and there would only encourage the Arabs to threaten more and more action, until, overcome by their own propaganda, they would try to invade Israel.

I know it is easy, with the calm precision of hindsight, to forget that the atmosphere of mounting tension and hysteria affected people's judgment in those weeks—my own, incidentally, included. But it seems evident that there *was* an alternative to fighting which was not seriously considered by the Israelis. What, after all, could have happened if Israel had stayed her hand? It is almost certain that the Arab frontier provocations would have increased and the clamour in Cairo and Damascus would have grown louder. But where would it have taken them? If it had been Israel's bluff that had been called first, when she did not immediately retaliate, it would have been the Arabs' bluff that would have been called second, when they had to face up to the fact that they were not capable of a full-scale attack on Israel. The most likely outcome, in fact, would have been that the crisis would have defused itself over a period of time, given some willingness among participants not to step over the brink.

But it never appeared to occur to the Israeli leadership to treat the subject as a political issue which required a political rather than a military approach. The possibility that the crisis would be defused, or at least carried over the critical period of tension, by some political gesture, say over the refugee issue, was not contemplated. And yet the whole dispute between Israel and the Arabs is littered with unresolved political issues—refugees, the Jordan waters, the rights of navigation, and so on—which belie the argument that the only ground left on which to start a dialogue was a battleground.

If the dispute was so barren then, what made it any less barren after the fighting? The only difference between the two situations was that Israel after the fighting held a position of supreme military dominance, whereas before, although still strategically stronger than her neighbours, she had at least temporarily lost the tactical initiative.

There is no doubting that Israel is an impatient nation. It was strange to find such a resourceful people so ready to accept that in most situations in their argument with the Arabs there was no alternative but to use force. Israel's technical, social and economic achievements are outstanding compared to those of her neighbours. Yet she does not appear to have progressed any more than the Arabs have in political terms. Why is this so? I believe that Israel's whole posture of militancy stems from the fact that the country was born in war, and it seems to have been the easiest way to maintain the national identity and the national momentum against a general background of war.

Twenty years after independence, Israel could afford to feel much more secure than she allows her society to believe. Israel had reached a kind of plateau in her development; some of the dynamism had gone out of her society and maybe no better ways to restimulate it had been found than by reference to the siege mentality which I have mentioned earlier. I am not qualified to suggest the psychological reasons for this attitude but in political terms it cannot help the prospect of peace through conciliation and *mutual* concessions by the two sides. The permanent military censorship of newspapers, the fact that the country's present leadership is the same group of people who fought their way to independence, the para-military settlements, all contribute to a society which, if not obsessed with security, nevertheless, places more emphasis on security than almost any other national aim. Few voices query whether there is the need for quite so much militancy. Questions affecting the further evolution and development of Israeli society—questions such as immigration affecting the future of the nation itself—are frequently ducked altogether or become sidetracked in the name of military security.

The tragedy of the 1967 crisis was that it was a repetition of all the previous crises between Israel and the Arabs, yet few of the protagonists seemed to care that they had all been there before, and, far from learning the lesson of history, appeared merely to have ignored or misinterpreted its mistakes. The dispute is treated as a military affair between the two sides, because the Arabs cannot exercise any political influence on Israel and therefore resort to force, and because Israel refuses to consider any political change in the area on the grounds that it would endanger her national security. These are both false positions. But as long as it *is* treated simply as a military argument, and the real political issues are ignored, there is every possibility of the same ritual of folly being gone through again.

8

The Future

THE WAR brought great territorial gains for Israel. She conquered the whole of the Sinai peninsula, including Sharm-el-Sheikh at the mouth of the Gulf of Aqaba and the whole of Jordanian Palestine. The Israeli army was in firm control from the east bank of the Suez canal to the west bank of the Jordan. The Syrian heights were conquered, the Syrian artillery positions blown up, and the Israeli forward positions could almost look down on the plain leading to Damascus.

Israel destroyed the Arab air forces, took possession of much abandoned equipment, decimated the enemy's capacity, and confirmed beyond reasonable doubt that she was the dominant military power in the Middle East. The possibility of that dominance being altered by the re-equipment of the Arab armies with more Soviet weapons has been raised alternately by the Arabs, to boost their morale, and by the Israelis to prevent complacency.

It is a threat without much foundation from either point of view. On the ground, Israel military power is one of the facts of life in the Middle East. I believe it would be a pity if the 1967 crisis was artificially concluded with a half-hearted solution based on the supposed necessity to guarantee Israel's security. As I have attempted to show, Israel's military security has not been seriously at issue, and now Israel must be one of the more secure countries in that neighbourhood. If any agreements were to be reached simply on the basis of a physical guarantee for Israel, they would overlook all the other fundamental differences which continue to exist between the two sides.

If Israel's basic security were the only necessary ingredient of a solution, then a formula could possibly be found whereby the Sinai desert, the Syrian heights and the west bank of the Jordan were all demilitarised. Israel would then be insulated on every frontier from the unwelcome attention of her Arab neighbours, and could hardly ask for more.

In fact, there would be flaws even in this arrangement. Assuming that the Arabs would not agree to the demilitarised areas being administered by Israel, then who would administer them? Would they be under UN administration, or a new Mandate Power? The Arabs would be unlikely to surrender their ultimate sovereignty over the areas to anybody else. Yet if they did not, they would always be in a position, in the final analysis, to evict the UN forces much as Egypt did in May 1967. This would presumably be treated as an act of war by Israel, which would bring us back to square one.

Besides, the mere fact of demilitarisation would not, of itself, guarantee that isolated guerrilla operations, or individual acts of terrorism across those frontiers, would stop. Israel would then be in the familiar position of having to retaliate indirectly for these acts, presumably outside the demilitarised zones, and the dangerous dialogue of terrorism and retaliation would start all over again.

It would also be hard to reach a simple settlement between Israel and the other littoral states which would solve the problem of freedom of navigation in the Gulf of Aqaba. It is tied up with the general problem of navigation through straits or narrows between the high seas, or between territorial waters, and one cannot imagine—indeed one should not imagine—a situation in which Egypt would sign away, under any conditions, all her rights to control shipping passing through the straits of Tiran. Yet anything short of that could obviously be revised and adjusted by Egypt, leading once again in that event to a position where Israel might claim such an act to be a *casus belli* whether or not it was arguable in law.

The military security of a nation which has shown that she can—even without international guarantees or assistance—completely dominate her neighbours should not be allowed to occupy our minds to the exclusion of the other issues in the dispute. Any settlement which was based merely on the achievement of such a guarantee would simply be a reversion to a political situation being similar to that which existed before the fighting. An opportunity to make a really radical attempt to solve some of the points of contention would have been thrown away. A reversion to that position would have solved nothing except Israel's territorial military security.

Yet even that formula would be incomplete in the sense that it would be forced to ignore the unchangeable facts of geography and the jet age. Supersonic aircraft tend to put the whole business of frontier security and frontier agreements into rather a false perspective. No formal guarantee could alter the fact that the cities of Israel and most of her Arab neighbours are only a few minutes away from each other as the modern bomber flies. So an agreement which simply attended to Israel's frontier security would signify a positive decision to solve only what Israel considered to be the most important part of the situation, while ignoring the other indivisible parts of the dispute.

A solution to the refugee problem is essential not only because of their plight but because without it one would avoid any final determination of the position which Israel will occupy within the Arab world. It is the nature of that position which at present contains the elements of combustion. It is the nature of Israel's position as an outpost, or as something apart from rather than in and of the world immediately around her, which seems to arouse such animosities in the Middle East.

It is tempting, indeed almost irresistible as a Western European to be fascinated, impressed, and to some extent caught up in the great experiment of Israel. Perhaps a Britisher's admiration reflects the repressed or frustrated colonialist influences still at work in Britain, since Israel almost by definition is the perfect example of colonialism at its best, as Theodor Herzl intended that it should be. Whatever it is, when one travels to the Middle East and finds a dynamic, cultured and intensely democratic country like Israel, one's sympathies go out to it. For a Western European, Israel certainly appears to be an outpost of our civilisation, and a shining example of what Western civilisation can achieve in that climate and on that land.

It is not only that the Israelis are a highly technical people; it is not only that they have achieved such agricultural success, visibly presented by the pleasing spectacle of forests rising on the formerly eroded hills west of Jerusalem, and the neat pattern of reclamation in the desert. It is also their great culture which has, after all, enriched European life during the centuries of the Jewish dispersion and which now, concentrated in a national context, is all the more impressive. It is the fusion of many Jewish sub-cultures brought in from the various communities both in and outside Europe which give a kind of kaleidoscopic aspect to a society which yet remains so obviously united. It is, perhaps above all, the fascinating achievement of the language of Hebrew, undeniably Israel's national language and now the first language of her citizens, although most of them were probably brought up and educated in some other language.

All these things seem to emphasise the stark contrast between modern Israel and the Arabs, and which condition many Western minds into believing that any nation which possesses such characteristics—so obviously superior to its neighbours—cannot very well be in the wrong. But though there is no moral issue about this, I believe that nations as a whole have to accept that their behaviour cannot be totally isolated from their neighbours. A nation has a choice either to adjust itself to the general pattern of the regional community to which it belongs (even Britain has been having trouble adjusting to the European Community) or else to accept the consequences, one of which might be expulsion or ostracism from that community, while another might be the subjugation of the community by the so called 'outsider' who would then force the other members to adjust themselves to it.

Without an adjustment of some kind, however, there will be no natural balance and instead there is likely to be the kind of regional tension, one way or the other, which exists between Israel and the Arab states even before one starts looking for specific issues which divide them. It exists because Israel is strong, Westernised, co-ordinated, volubly political and yet united, in an area where the Arabs are seldom these things, and instinctively resent the presence among them of one who is so different.

It is no good pretending that because the Jews are allegedly descended from Isaac and the Arabs from his brother Ishmael they are therefore all part of the same family, with similar characteristics. As far as the great mass of European originated Jews are concerned, that is not so. They are more Russian, more Polish, or more German than they are Middle Eastern, and few of them could have known or heard much about the Arabs until they emigrated to Israel.

Israel is not a Middle Eastern state—yet. But it is true that those very Jews who came from central and Eastern Europe are worried that it might turn into one eventually by the high birth rate, not so much of the 300,000 strong Arab minority within Israel, but of the Oriental Jews who came to Israel from Arab countries like Iraq, Morocco, Yemen and who are definitely more Middle Eastern in character than they are European. At present they are not only in a minority, but have little influence or participation in the leadership of the country. Their general standards are lower than those of European extraction. They may be raised up to correspond more closely to the Europeans, but it is just as likely that over a period of time they will by dint of their numerical majority within the society gradually impose their own stamp on Israel, away from the character of a small eastern European state which it has today and more towards a Middle Eastern one.

This possibility reveals the internal contradiction within Israel. It is one of the causes for the plateau in the nation's development which had been reached before the 1967 crisis, with questions about the way forward left unresolved and possibly unresolvable.

Israel was born as a Jewish state. That Jewishness is underwritten by one of the basic laws, the Law of Return, which grants automatic citizenship to any Jew who comes to Israel. It is based on the dubious legality that Jews the world over have an inherent right to a kind of dual citizenship between Israel and their country of adoption, if they feel so inclined. It also carries with it a moral obligation on Jews outside Israel to return to their homeland, although this obligation goes expressly against both the letter and the spirit of the Balfour declaration. This pressure is sometimes actively argued by Israelis on the grounds that another round of persecutions of the Jews, in their own countries such as Western Europe or the United States, may be only just around the corner, and they should return to their homeland before it is too late.

Israel's population increased to the present level largely because of the immigration of Jews whose situation in their lands of origin was thought to be worse, and probably was worse, than it would be in Israel, where they would be neither a persecuted minority nor a separate community but, by their very Jewishness, they would establish their common identity with the rest of the nation. The contradiction, or at least the dilemma, for Israel, came when that immediate source of immigration ran out; when, with one exception, the Jewish communities elsewhere in the world presumably were able to decide for themselves that they were better off where they were than they would be if they moved to Israel, many having assimilated successfully into their own countries in Western Europe, the United States, or South Africa.

Israel does not stop actively canvassing for new citizens from these quarters, and moral pressure is put on them to return, or if not to return at least to donate funds to Israel to atone for their staying away. This accounts for the tremendous volume of funds which finds its way into Israel in times of crisis, and during the 1967 emergency it is said to have reached the astonishing figure of 500 million dollars. The one exception to all this is Russian Jewry, which has become a kind of talisman for Israel.

There is evidence that Soviet Jews are sometimes actively discriminated against in the Soviet Union, and the Israeli assumption is that, if the Russian Jews were given a choice between emigrating to Israel and staying in Russia, an appreciable part of their two and a half million number would opt for Israel.

Even if only 100,000 did so it would bring a much needed increase to Israeli society, where immigration has fallen right off during the last few years. But the chances of the Soviet Government jeopardising its relationship with the Arab states by allowing any Jewish immigration of this scale are so slim as to be almost non-existent.

Although the economic and defence needs of Israel may not

urgently require more population, it is obvious that a general increase in its population would improve the country's performance, and it would particularly help Israel if that increase was made up of technically qualified people with a high standard of education or a high potential—in fact a brain gain. Moreover, as a proportion of the population as a whole, the number of technically qualified and educated people in Israel is now falling off, as the number of Oriental immigrants has increased. Unless some outside element is introduced, the general standard of Israel, and therefore presumably her performance, will become less dynamic than it has been during her first twenty years.

In the early 1960s Israel's population was growing at the average annual rate of about 3·6 per cent, two per cent of which was in immigration, and only 1·6 per cent through natural increase. Now that immigration has tailed off—there may indeed have been a net *emigration* during 1965 and 1966—the natural increase obviously acquired greater significance, and a breakdown of the figures into categories of national origin is disturbing to people who would like Israeli society to preserve its present European bias.

The country's 300,000 Arabs average eight children to a family; Jews from Morocco, Yemen and other Oriental countries average five; the native born Israelis produce 2·7 children, and the European and American originated families average barely two children each. It is the message of these figures which drives the Israeli to hunt elsewhere in order to redress this automatic trend which will otherwise continue unchecked. It could only be corrected by a really large influx of Jews with a European background which is why Israel casts such a forlorn eye at the tantalisingly large community in Russia.

Israelis seem to believe that Soviet Jews—unlike their more apathetic American and Western European cousins—would respond to the appeal to return if they were only allowed to do so. As it is, Israel is faced with the prospect of emigration increasing among her most qualified people if the ethnic standards in the country, in their opinion, continue to deteriorate as the figures suggest. Once emigration of these people starts, it automatically has an adverse effect on immigration as well, and the whole trend would threaten to become a cumulative decrease in the most valued categories of population.

The Arabs would ask this question: if the Israelis really want and need more people in their country why are they looking elsewhere in the world when there are more than one million homeless Palestinians still in the area? The Israelis would answer that they were not Jews. But do they have to be Jews? Does the absolutely uncompromising nature of Israel's Jewishness really mean that no non-Jewish immigrant is acceptable to Israel in spite of her wants and needs?

I know there are practical reasons why many of the Palestinian refugees would not be reabsorbed into Israel, and why Israel is reluctant to take in a more backward community of people in much the same way as Britain is reluctant to receive more than a limited number of certain categories of immigrants from the Commonweatlh. But Israel has never acknowledged the principle of allowing the return of any of them.

Although the implementation of any such principle would be hard, nobody believes that, in practice, it would have to extend very far. But it is the principle of exclusiveness which Israel practises to a greater extent than any other nation today—with the possible exception of South Africa—which certainly acts as one of the major irritants in the Middle East. Israel was founded as a Jewish state, and its laws and customs are essentially Jewish. The Balfour declaration provided for a Jewish community, and the UN partition agreement provided for two half countries representing the Jewish and Arab communities, joined in an economic union. But Israelis now say that only through statehood could the Jewish community be certain of guaranteeing their existence, and that nothing else could be 'secured in public law'. Therefore they would see any erosion of that statehood, such as might come about by an ethnic trend which eventually led to the Jews being a minority, as a threat to their community as a whole and so to their ultimate existence. The Israelis argue that as Jews they have been a minority group long enough, and they are now determined to remain a majority, even if it means keeping out the real majority by force.

If that is the argument, and I have heard it many times, then one must look carefully at a crucial decision taken during the 1967 emergency, which was taken on military grounds alone but which nevertheless contained profound political implications for the future of Israel. That was the decision, not simply to neutralise the Jordanian attacks on Israel, but to sweep the whole way through Jordanian Palestine and occupy the entire area between Israel and the west bank of the river. It was a plan which had obvious military advantages at the time, because it not only secured the line of hills overlooking Israel, which had long been coveted by the Israeli military, and from which Jordanian frontier incursions had been launched, but it also meant that Israel could seize a little extra territory as well—between those hills and the Jordan—which would come in useful as a bargaining counter in post-war negotiations.

The decision was taken by the Israeli war cabinet on the first morning of the war. It was taken on the prompting of the Chief of Staff, General Rabin, whose advice on that first day of war was liable to carry extra weight. Were the rest of the Israeli ministers aware then, however, that this decision—though presented as a tactical military issue—actually had enormous political consequences for Israel which would probably dwarf all previous decisions that had been made in their first twenty years? They may have thought they were, in a stroke, knocking out the Palestine problem by taking the remainder of Palestine from Jordan. But in the same stroke they were absorbing the Palestine problem themselves, in that the refugees problem then became automatically an internal problem for Israel. It was thereafter within the area of her own physical control and responsibility, whereas before she had disclaimed both political and physical responsibility for the refugees.

However much in the past Israel had disclaimed responsibility for the rehabilitation of refugees, her own physical occupation since 1967 of territory wherein they reside has made it all the more urgent for her to see that the problem is solved and she can thus hardly avoid assuming some political interest in the issue as well.

But there were even deeper implications in the decision.

Because there were not only refugees living on the west bank, but also a large population of Palestinians who had lived there for a very long time, and had not been uprooted by the 1948 war because they were already living in territory which had never been disputed, they could not then be treated as refugees: for how long could Israel treat them as a captive people? The difference between the acquisition of Jordan's west bank and the capture and retention of Gaza and the Syrian heights was that Israel could feasibly retain the latter areas and subject them to direct military rule since the resident populations there were either small or consisted largely of refugees who would anyway have been organised under a military aegis.

But that could hardly become a permanent condition for Israeli rule over the west bank of Jordan, mainly because of the numbers involved, but also because of the nature of the people themselves. Of the one and a half million people situated on the west bank, less than half—about 600,000—were refugees. The remainder could hardly be treated differently from Israel's own Arabs if Israel's occupation of that area was to be a long one. Although Israel's own Arabs had been subjected to military rule and had to suffer various kinds of discrimination for nearly 20 years, they had little by little been able to improve their lot and become much more integrated citizens in Israel than they had been to start with.

That is not to suggest that they were indistinguishable from the Jews in Israel because that would not be true. They are still discriminated against in some fields of employment, and they have fewer educational opportunities than other Israelis but they are probably nearly as well off now in most respects, in Israel, even as Arabs, as they would be anywhere else.

The capture of the west bank seemed to present the Israelis with a variety of alternative policies in the period after the war. They could hand back all that territory which was not directly relevant to their frontier security, in exchange for certain political concessions from the Arabs, such as diplomatic recognition, another more binding ceasefire agreement and probably the complete avoidance of any discussion about the refugees. This would hardly have been a formula for a long-term peace, because peace between Israel and the Arabs does not depend simply either on Israel's frontier security or official recognition of her existence by the Arabs, although the latter could help to make subsequent negotiations between them much easier. Although even this agreement would initially be quite politically unacceptable to the Arabs, Israel thought she could achieve it simply by hanging on to the captured territory until the Arabs had to come forward and talk. Whether or not it would find favour with the Arabs, it is the sort of agreement which represents about the minimum acceptable to the people of Israel themselves. They can hardly be expected so soon after their victory—and the Arab aggression which they believe preceded it—voluntarily to swallow any agreement which did not appear to be patently to their advantage.

Another possible settlement which has been aired in Israel is to return to Egypt and Syria those parts of the captured territory which could be returned without military insecurity. The remainder would then be demilitarised, and an Arab protectorate would be set up on the west bank—a self-governing Arab satrapy whose foreign affairs and defence would be run by Israel, and whose economy would benefit from the infusion of Israeli capital and technology, while Israel herself would benefit from the larger home market and a much shorter outside frontier to defend. One shortcoming of such an arrangement, however, is that it ignores the refugee problem. They presumably would continue to be corralled into camps in Gaza and on the west bank, and encouraged to emigrate to Arab countries where once again they would become centres of dissidence.

Another disadvantage is that such an arrangement would appear to underline the superiority of the Jews over the Arabs and would formally institutionalise it in a way which I do not believe would be politically possible or acceptable to the remainder of the Arab world—even if it was militarily impossible for them to do anything about it. They could, as in the past, always do just enough about the position to stimulate unrest, and the history of protest in the Arab world has shown how easy it is, with the aid of one or two grenade incidents, to crystallise opposi-

tion to a state of affairs, and induce terrorism as a means of articu-
lating that opposition.

I am not suggesting that Israel has any moral responsibility to
avoid giving this impression of superiority over the Arabs, but I
believe that she must now face the fact in the Middle East that if
she does carry out policies which upset the Arabs, she alone has
the responsibility for living with that hostility both in the short
and long term. The Arabs have as much right to object to her
policies as she has to carry them out, even if they have no actual
power to make their objections felt. But the irritating ingredient
of this protectorate proposal lies more in the way it would
formally recognise and substantiate Israeli dominance over Arab
Palestine, by the setting up of a puppet state, than in the fact
that Israel was strong enough to do so.

Is there any other way, therefore, of arriving at a solution to
the dispute which would keep the two parts of Palestine together,
which is, I believe, the only basis on which there may be eventual
peace?

I believe that such a condition could be achieved, but covertly,
not the subject of any formal understanding, in fact rather the
reverse in that it would be the product of years, a decade maybe,
or even a generation or two of further impasse and possible
discord between the two sides, and I shall attempt to explain how.

Israel is a democracy. Her Government is democratically
elected and the ability of that Government to trample on the
carefully cultured instincts of the people of Israel is therefore
very circumscribed. We know, in the main, what those instincts
are. They are to keep Israel a strong independent and Jewish
state. The concessions involved in reaching either of the first
two possible settlements I have mentioned would amount to
about the limit of Israeli tolerance if they were to continue to
feel that their ambitions and instincts were being observed.

One would indeed find many quarters in Israel who would
argue that there was no point in retreating at all from the present
position. They would argue that the Arabs by their aggression
asked for all that they received, and that if Israel can now maintain her position why should she not do so. But generally speaking
I think we can take it that any solution which fitted in with the

instincts of the Israeli people would be inadequate in terms of political satisfaction to the Arabs. They might be forced to accept it, but unwilling acceptance of a situation under duress is something with which the Arabs have been quite familiar during the last forty years of Palestine's history, and there is no sign yet that they are ready to bow to *force majeure*.

Israel appears to hope for a change of heart this time, but I believe that such a change of heart will not, indeed cannot, come until there is a change in the internal political identity of Israel itself. The difficulty lies in the fact that any such change within Israel would have to be an involuntary one, because it would totally undermine the present principle of a Zionist state.

It must first be made clear that the world can neither ask nor expect the Government voluntarily to commit suicide by agreeing to any settlement which flouted the principles on which the state is based. Whatever one may think of these principles, and however responsible for the present state of affairs one may consider them, they are nevertheless securely based in law, and upheld by an elected and internationally recognised government. Moreover the Israeli Government with the nation behind it at present has the power to insist on the retention of those exclusive features of their society even if they attract the hostility of peoples around them.

Israel has shown that, in the final analysis, she is powerful enough to neutralise that hostility. I do not think, therefore, that it is possible, particularly in the aftermath of victory, for the Israeli Government to agree to any settlement in the area which could contain anything like the minimum ingredient of compromise required to satisfy the Arabs. They are thinking along totally different lines, but there is nothing the Arabs can do. Israeli power cannot be successfully challenged now, and I doubt whether it could be in the foreseeable future, no matter what new equipment is delivered to the Arabs. So long as Israel retains first of all the ability to hit back—and that will always be guaranteed to her by the United States to balance off any Soviet arms deliveries to the Arabs—and secondly her possession of her present frontiers, she can present her neighbours with a very real threat of invasion leading to *their* collapse, if they overdo their hostility to her.

How can this difficulty be resolved? How could the people of Israel, so wary of change, and so ready to rule out as unacceptable any development which undermined their Zionists' principles, nevertheless be induced to accept a new situation in Palestine which did not merit the hostility of the Arabs? Does the world have to face the prospects of enduring another long period of strife and frustration in the Middle East before a settlement could be achieved? I believe that we do. We have already endured two generations, and it may well be another two generations before there is much chance of the dispute being satisfactorily settled. Is there any way it could be settled other than the Arabs eventually overrunning Israel and causing a dispersion comparable to the original dispersion when Jerusalem was sacked? I regard that prospect as inconceivable with more than two-and-a-half million Jews now in Israel. On the other hand I do not believe any solution to the problem is possible without Palestine being treated as a single entity, and without a much closer relationship between the two races within it than is contemplated today.

That may sound heresy to the Zionists and propagators of a purely theocratic state in Israel. It may sound inconceivable to those who say that under no conditions can the two races come closer, whose experience of Palestine under the Mandate, or the West Bank since the 1967 occupation, has convinced them that Jewish and Arab communities can only work together if there is some higher authority over them to see that they do.

I question this view profoundly. People used to say that about Christian and Muslim, and yet it is a more or less working partnership in the Lebanon next door, in spite of the fact that the historical differences between Christian and Muslim have been far more terrible than they were between Jew and Arab. People now say that Greek and Turk are incompatible in Cyprus, and yet this incompatibility is a new creation, unknown less than fifty years ago when they lived quite compatibly side by side.

I believe that the only possibility for an equitable settlement to the Arab-Israel problem lies in the opportunity inadvertently provided by the Israeli capture of the West Bank of the Jordan. For the first time since 1948 Palestine is an entity again, and I personally would welcome the failure of any settlement which again divided the two parts of Palestine, because I do not think it could last. Thus I would hope that no formula can be agreed which would concentrate solely on the artificial issue of Israel's military security or her recognition by the Arab world. The opportunity once more available is to treat the future of Palestine as a whole, whereas before one had to accept the artificial division between Jordan on the one hand and Israel on the other which automatically gave two unreconcilable attitudes to the same problem. In treating the problem in this way the other individual points of contention such as the Jordan waters and the fate of the Palestinian refugees should fall a little more easily into place—though the ultimate future of Transjordan would have to hinge on some arrangement between Iraq, Syria and Saudi Arabia.

Obviously the ideal would be a binational state in Israel where the Jewish community could preserve its dynamism without being engulfed by the Arabs, even by an Arab majority, but where the refugees could also be rehabilitated and the economic affairs of the area—including water resources—treated as one.

The success of such an arrangement might hinge on the question whether or not the dynamism of the Israelis could first of all exist without that particular extra stimulus which it has received from nationhood, and if that was possible, then secondly whether it could do so without inspiring the defensive hostility of those Arabs who, though not part of it, nevertheless would be closely enough involved to feel uncomfortable about its force.

There seems to be no reason why all the impressive elements in Israel should be lost if that country became part of a Middle Eastern state—a binational state—or even an Arab state with a large Jewish minority within it. Over a period of a generation or two, the ethnic developments suggest that the Oriental Jews and the Arabs together will outnumber the Jews from Europe. It is inconceivable that the nature of Israel would not change to reflect that trend. Hitherto the Jews have been able to keep the

Arabs out, but it would be a different matter to hold them down.

This may, of course, result in an increased emigration among those Jews in Israel who delight in the modernity and sophistication—the Westernisation—of their state, just as we Europeans probably delight in it when we go there. But if a natural balance in the essentially Arab Middle East is more likely to be achieved through the presence of a less Westernised Israel, we should surely assist in that process or at least keep our disappointments to ourselves, rather than help to delay the change by pro-Israeli and anti-Arab propaganda, or through fear that such an attitude might be construed as anti-semitism. I think, therefore, it would be a pity if the West Bank was returned to Jordan, and I hope the Arabs do not present Israel with the kind of apparently tempting offer which might encourage her to trade the West Bank, or part of it, in exchange for some guarantee.

But if no such settlement is forthcoming, Israel would therefore be forced to assume responsibility for the entire West Bank in a way for which she is eminently equipped, if she can be prepared to do so. That kind of responsibility will have a widening effect on Israel's horizons. The economic integration of the West Bank with Israel which would have to come—and is already beginning to come—could not fail to be followed by the development of a much closer integration over the years.

At present there is the regular exchange of fire with Jordan across the river, but these outbursts are more expressions of Jordanian impotence than serious preparations for war. Israel can handle them just as she is able—at a cost—to handle the increased security work brought on by the absorption of one-and-a-half million potentially hostile Arabs into her area of control. But unless total apartheid is to be practised on the Arabs by the Israelis—and one can see how even South Africa is finding it hard to maintain the totality of that approach—the trickle of inconsistency over a generation would become a torrent. Assisted by economic factors which would make it progressively harder to separate the two parts of Palestine, the area would not be able to avoid a closer cohesion, even if in practice this still meant that the two communities very much kept to their own areas. It would be hard, for instance, to prevent traffic developing between the two parts, and even marginal shifts of populations as economic factors came into play and demand for more industrial labour here, or more agriculture there, made racial and territorial distinctions much harder to maintain.

The crucial element in such a situation would obviously concern the status of citizens in the occupied areas. Politically this would be a field of mounting pressure. For an initial period the role of military occupation would presumably banish political thoughts from most Arabs' minds—but not entirely. The possibility of their co-operation would, I believe, be hindered under these circumstances if the situation was formalised through any kind of variant on the protectorate proposal.

The Palestinian Arabs would be more likely to accept this situation if it was not officially forced down their throats by any kind of written agreement testifying to their collaboration, which would be an easy instrument for other more hostile elements in the Arab world to use against them. It took twenty years for Israel's own Arabs to achieve something approaching comparability with the Jews; how much less time would it take the Palestinians in their greater numbers and great political cohesion, to force political concessions from the Israeli Government? If Israel had decided to retain Jordan's West Bank, she would have simultaneously to decide that the best way to maintain control was through a largely collaborationist population, and not a hostile one, and that collaboration by the Arabs would presumably command a price.

This may all appear to be a highly improbable line of thought. It may in fact appear to be vitiated in the short term by an agreement between Israel and the Arabs after a few more months of spasmodic frontier sniping, which yet would do nothing to solve the basic difference between them. The period after the 1956 Suez campaign started in exactly the same way, with bold declarations from various quarters, particularly in Israel, saying that things would never be the same again. It took five months to wear down these good intentions and induce the Israelis to give up their captured territory in Sinai in exchange for the UN force and the American guarantees over the Gulf. In those five months, too, the Arab position was subject to the same kind of shifts and spasms as it is now, as the leaders continue to plan their anti-Israel policy almost in a vacuum.

I can see no valid short-term formula, however, which will really prevent another crisis recurring. I can only hope that there will not be one. The prospect of unresolved tension for the next decade may seem to be a high price to pay for the possibility that at the end of the period, the Arabs may have discovered that Israel has inadvertently de-Zionised herself by the enforced absorption of such a large Arab population. Anyone who believes it is too high should remember that no amount of diplomacy in the past has managed to prevent the Palestine problem being endemic to Middle East tensions in some form or another for the last forty years. We should not expect to exorcise those ghosts so soon.